Parent's and Kid's Complete Guide to Summer Camp Fun

Parent's and Kid's Complete Guide to Summer Camp Fun

Everything You Need to Prepare for an Incredible Camp Adventure!

Penny Warner

PRIMA PUBLISHING

Published by Prima Publishing, Roseville, California. Member of the Crown Publishing Group, a division of Random House, Inc.

PRIMA PUBLISHING and colophon are trademarks of Random House, Inc., registered with the United States Patent and Trademark Office.

Illustrations by Charles Stubbs

Library of Congress Cataloging-in-Publication Data
Warner, Penny.
    Parent's and kid's complete guide to summer camp fun :
everything you need to prepare for an incredible camp
adventure! / Penny Warner
      p.   cm.
    Includes index.
    ISBN 0-7615-3746-5
    1. Camps. I. Title.
    GV192.W37   2002

796.54'2—dc21   2002022001

02 03 04 05 DD 10 9 8 7 6 5 4 3 2 1
Printed in the United States of America

First Edition

Visit us online at www.primapublishing.com

To my happy campers,
Tom, Matthew, and Rebecca

Contents

Acknowledgments ix

Introduction xi

Part I: Parent's Guide

1. Camp Havalotta Fun

Choosing the Right Camp for Your Child 3

2. Countdown to Camp

Preparing Your Child Emotionally for the Adventure . . . 28

3. Packin' Up

What to Pack for Camp and Send Along for Fun 49

4. Heading Off and Coming Home

Getting Your Child to Camp Safely and Happily 93

Part II: Kid's Guide

5. Your First Day
Dealing with Homesickness 109

6. Tent Fun
Activities, Games, and Gags 119

7. Over the Coals
Snazzy Campfire Snacks 139

8. Gather Together for Fun!
Great Group Games and Activities 146

9. Make It Yourself
Camp Arts and Crafts 158

10. Into the Wilderness
Nature Know-How 170

11. Wish You Were Here
Letters to Home 181

12. Dear Diary . . .
Filling Your Journal Pages 189

13. Note to Campers
Safety and Basic First Aid 194

Index 203

Acknowledgments

Thanks to my contributors, Erin Ambrose, Kaveh Amini, Deb Bargas, Marie-Elena Bartra, Charu Bhardwaj, Colleen Casey, Vanessa Hodge, Priscilla Hopkins, Maureen Gin, Francesca Marie Graves, Melody Johnson, Nancy Kindley, Dave Krumboltz, Christy Kuhner, Teresa Lau, Josh Littlefield, Tamara Mader, Steve and Kelly Magoon, Colleen Miller, Candy Nauman, Ann Parker, Kristina Schultz, Barbara Shabaniani, Vicki Stadelhofer, Tracy Stotka, Pat Tracy, Sue Warner, Susan Westerlund, Dina Willner, and Allie Young. And a special thanks to Jamie Miller, my wonderful editor.

Introduction

Going to summer camp is an exciting adventure and wonderful opportunity for kids. It's a chance to get away from home, learn interesting skills, meet new friends, and experience a stimulating environment. The benefits of being independent, gaining confidence, and increasing competency usually far outweigh any negatives that may accompany going to camp.

But it's also a scary time for some kids, who are away from their parents for the first time. They may miss their friends, pets, bedrooms, and even their sisters and brothers. Some kids feel lonely just the first days of camp, while a few may experience homesickness for most of the session.

So while the rewards are great, your child may still have concerns about leaving home and being on his own. His fears and feelings about homesickness are real, and they need to be acknowledged and understood. As a parent, you want to help your child experience the most fulfilling and enjoyable time at camp possible.

Parent's and Kid's Complete Guide to Summer Camp Fun was created for this purpose: to help parents prepare their kids for the camping experience and to help kids make the transition from home to camp stress-free, easy, and fun. I've divided the book into two sections, a Parent's Guide (begins on page 1) and a Kid's Guide (begins on page 107), so there are information and tips for both you and your child.

The Parent's Guide includes everything a parent needs to know about sending a child to camp, from choosing the right camp, preparing for the trip, and packing the suitcase to helping the young camper adjust to a new environment, make new friends, and cope with homesickness.

The Kid's Guide offers games and songs, activities, nature fun, arts and crafts, night time entertainment, campfire fun, staying safe, dealing with homesickness, and boredom busters to keep your child occupied every minute of the day and evening.

Best of all, *Parent's and Kid's Complete Guide to Summer Camp Fun* will keep your child so busy, she won't have time to feel lonely, bored, or homesick. So roll up the sleeping bag, pack the knapsack, and check the flashlight batteries, and then stuff a copy of *Parent's and Kid's Complete Guide to Summer Camp Fun* into the backpack for the best camp experience of a lifetime!

Part I

Parent's Guide

You probably bought this book because you've been thinking about sending your child to camp. Perhaps you spent one or more summers at camp as a child and still have fond memories of the experience. You want the same for your child but don't know exactly where to begin. You may have more questions and concerns as a parent than you ever did as a child preparing for the big adventure. Is my child ready for camp? What kind of camp would my child enjoy? Where do I find a good camp? Perhaps you don't even know what questions to ask. Well, we've got the questions *and* the answers, right here in the parents' guide. So let's get you started in the right direction.

1

Camp
Havalotta Fun

Choosing the Right Camp
for Your Child

More than seven million children go to overnight camp every year. Will your child be one of them? Before you start looking for a camp that suits your child's needs and interests, you might want to make sure he's ready for the camp experience. Many experts feel the ideal age for camp is around 9 or 10 years. But not all children are ready at the same time, so age isn't always a factor. Then how do you know your child is ready? Here are some questions to consider.

Is Your Child Ready for Camp?

Go over the following questions to help you decide whether your child is ready for camp:

Has your child expressed an interest in camp? When you've talked with your child, has she mentioned the idea of going to camp or suggested a camping trip with the family? Has she asked to spend the night in the backyard or set up a tent to play in? These are signs that your child may be interested in going away to camp.

Is your child mature enough to handle camp? Most children under the age of seven are not ready to go away to camp, but sometimes older children aren't ready, either. More than age, your child's maturity level plays an important role in determining whether he's ready to leave home for a week or so. Does he spend the night away from home easily? Does he seem ready to separate from you for a day or so? If so, he may be ready to head for the hills.

Is your child independent and self-sufficient? Some children develop self-help skills early and can dress themselves, make their own lunches, and take care of their rooms without a lot of supervision, while other children seem to constantly rely on their parents for help. Does your child like to do things for herself, or is she still fairly dependent on you for the basics? Are her self-help skills improving over time, or has she been slow to develop these skills? The answers to these questions may help you determine whether your child needs another year or two before going to camp.

Is your child outgoing and able to speak up if he has a question or concern? Some children are too reserved to ask for what they need and may be overlooked in a crowd, while others aren't afraid to seek help if needed. Does your child ask his teacher questions when he doesn't understand something? Is he bold enough to talk to clerks and other adults in authority when he has a question? If not, it may be something you want to work on before he's on his own.

What Do You Want in a Camp for Your Child?

The next question you'll want to ask yourself—and your child—is what you both want in a camp. There are hundreds of different kinds of camps and camp experiences, and the choices may seem overwhelming. Some camps offer opportunities for children to learn leadership skills that help them grow into successful adults, while others may focus on helping kids avoid risky behaviors, such as drugs, alcohol, or violence. Since going to camp can often change a child's life, think about what you want your child to experience overall as well as specifically while at camp. Here are some general and specific options to discuss with your child to help you find the right camp.

Generally, what are you looking for in a camp for your child? The overall philosophy of the camp is important to think about before making a decision:

◆ Do you hope camp will help instill particular values or beliefs in your child?

◆ Are you interested in expanding your child's knowledge or skills?

◆ Do you want a change in your child's behavior or attitudes?

◆ Are you hoping to increase your child's social skills and friendships?

◆ Do you want your child to experience success and gain higher self-esteem?

◆ Do you hope your child will learn leadership skills and gain a sense of community from camp?

Specifically, what does your child want from camp? He'll be more likely to go to camp and enjoy the experience if it offers specific activities within his area of interest:

◆ Is your child looking for physical activity and skill building that sports such as baseball camp or rafting adventures may offer?

"I'll never forget the cool sounds and smells of nature—birds singing, smell of breakfast cooking, pine and clean air, the sheer beauty of nature. Remind your kids to notice their surroundings while they're there."

—*Pat T.*

- Does your child prefer a wide variety of activities to choose from, such as arts and crafts, nature studies, or outdoor adventures?
- Does your child want to learn something new or add to his growing knowledge of a subject, in areas like computer science, filmmaking, or space?
- Is there something specific your child is looking for in a camp?

Five Major Goals of Camp

Many camps offer opportunities for both overall growth and specific developmental skills, so you might look for those that combine them. Most of all, make sure the camp you choose offers what's most important to your child. Here are the five most common goals of camp for kids:

1. *Have fun!* Why else would a kid go to camp except to have a good time!
2. *Make new friends.* Your child will have the opportunity to increase his social skills and make a new set of friends.
3. *Learn something new.* Camps provide all kinds

of new learning experiences for your child in a wide variety of areas.

4. *Experience a new environment.* Your child has the chance to get away from home and find out what life is like in a new and different place.

5. *Survive!* Your child will find out he can survive away from his family, friends, and home. Sometimes that's the most important thing he'll take away from camp.

What Kinds of Camps Are Available for My Child?

If you search the Internet, you may be overwhelmed by the number and kinds of camps available. There are more than 8,500 day and resident camps in the United States alone. We've provided a fairly comprehensive list of camps here to show you the scope and variety of the camping opportunities for your child. You may be surprised at the diversity and specificity of camps; there's a different type of camp for almost every conceivable interest, which makes choosing the right camp so important—and sometimes so difficult.

Begin by thinking about what type of program the camp has to offer and whether it matches your child's personality type. Be sure to include your child in the decision-making process so that he feels he's a part of experience and has a say in the selection. Here are some of the choices you might have to consider.

Resident Camp Versus Day Camp

At a resident camp, your child will sleep overnight and stay for a period of one to eight weeks. He may be housed in a cabin, tent, or tepee during his stay, or he may sleep out-of-doors. Most resident camps offer supervised activities throughout the day and have a large staff to oversee the program. If your child goes to day camp, there are no sleeping quarters, so he's transported each morning and afternoon or evening by bus, van, or private car to the campsite and back.

Structured Versus Flexible Program

Some camps provide a structured environment for the campers, with every minute of the day and evening planned full of activities and programs. Other camps offer your child more flexibility, allowing her to choose what she wants to do and when she wants to do it. This also provides her with the opportunity to take a break if she feels tired or overstimulated.

Family Camps Versus Kids-Only Camps

You might want to go to camp as a family, which provides a vacation for all of you as well as an opportunity to spend time together. It might be the best choice for a first-time camp experience for your child. If you choose a kids-only camp, your child will have the chance to be independent and get along on his own, without the family around to supervise him.

Expensive Versus Reasonable Cost of Camp

The average cost of camp ranges from $15 to $80 a day, so there's a camp for every budget. Check to see whether the camp is run by a nonprofit agency, public agency, youth group, or private agency and what your tuition pays for, such as the staff, accommodations, food, supplies, and insurance. Some camps offer scholarships and assistance, and some give discounts if you enroll more than one child.

Specific Versus General Activities

Some camps specialize in one specific interest area, such as sports or science, while others offer a wide variety of choices so that there's something for everyone, especially those with many interests. Specific interest camps provide the opportunity to improve skills in one or two areas, while general interest camps give your child a well-rounded selection of activities to explore.

Short Versus Long Sessions

The length of the camp experience is important to consider since some children will be able to handle only a week away from home, while others will thrive in a longer program, perhaps up to eight weeks. Make sure your child understands the length of the session before signing him up.

Other Considerations Regarding Camp

Here are some other questions to ask yourself when looking for the right camp for your child. You might make a pros-and-cons list and check off the things that are important to you both:

◆ Are the children the same age as your child, or will there be a variety of ages together?

◆ Are there both male and female counselors, and what are their roles?

◆ Are the activities available to all ages, or are there age restrictions?

◆ Are the kids allowed to join their siblings in the activities, or are they kept separate?

◆ How does the staff deal with personal problems and other concerns your child might have?

◆ How is routine homesickness handled, and how is severe homesickness determined?

◆ Do the guidance and discipline techniques of the camp match your parenting style?

◆ Does the camp promote competition between children or cooperation among children, and which do you prefer for your child?

◆ What are the qualifications and background of the camp director?

◆ Is the ratio of staff at least one counselor to each six to eight campers?

- What are the ages of the staff, and are at least 80 percent over 18 years?
- Is there a high return rate in the staff—at least 50 percent?
- How are the special needs of the kids handled, such as necessary provisions, special facilities, medical staff, medicine dispensing, and distribution of special foods for dietary restrictions?
- Are behavior concerns handled in a positive manner, with positive reinforcement and positive role models?
- Does the camp send brochures or videos of the site, or can you visit ahead of time to get acquainted with the place?
- Are you allowed to visit the camp or make contact with your child during the session?
- How far from home is the camp, and is that a concern?
- Is the camp coed or same gender, and what are the benefits?
- What kind of living quarters are provided for the campers?
- Are there any hidden fees or extra costs for special activities?
- Do the campers need extra spending money while at camp?
- Is there a dining facility, and what does it provide, especially for picky eaters?
- Have there been any recent changes in the camp program, and why?
- Are there any special traditions the camp observes, such as holidays, birthday, or other camp-related observances?
- What kind of first aid, health facilities, and safety equipment does the camp provide?
- How is the camp set up for an emergency?

Specific Camps

Here are just some of the specific camps available for your child and what they have to offer.

Academic Camps

These camps offer an educational slant to the program and help kids build skills in academic areas. They strive to make learning fun while helping kids improve their knowledge, education, and skills:

> Archaeology camp: study bones, go on archaeological digs
> Business camp: learn business skills, accounting, management
> Computer camp: write software, programming, build Web sites
> History camp: Civil War reenactments, visit historical sites
> Language camp: learn French, Spanish, Italian, sign language
> Marine biology camp: study tide pools, oceans, marine life
> Math camp: improve math skills, play math games, careers
> Science camp: do experiments, learn theories, career information
> Writing camp: improve creative writing skills and expression

Art Camps

Art camps provide opportunities for kids to explore their creativity, engage in art experiences, and improve their art skills. Most art camps offer a wide variety of media to experiment with:

Arts and crafts camp: make crafts using a variety of materials

Film and video camp: use a camera, making a short film/video

Fine arts camp: painting, sculpting, other fine arts

Music camp: learn an instrument, appreciate music

Performing arts camp: acting, mime, performing, improvisation

Photography camp: taking and developing pictures

 Tip

Include a big plastic garbage bag for dirty clothes.

College/University Camps

Many of the nation's colleges and universities offer families and kids the opportunity to live on campus and attend special activities. These camps are often more affordable and less rustic than many other camps and provide an alternative to the wilderness style of camping.

Leadership Camps

Kids learn how to work with others, form groups, provide direction, make decisions, and enhance self-confidence. Often a symbolic government is formed where kids practice running for office, voting, creating measures, and working toward the good of the people.

Military Camps

If your child has an interest in the military, he'll have the opportunity to participate in military maneuvers and rise in the ranks within a structured and disciplined environment.

Religious/Church Camps

You may want to provide your child with a religious-based experience where the camp activities and philosophy fit the beliefs and values of the family as well as the child.

Scout Camps

If your child belongs to a scouting organization, you may want to investigate a camp specifically for Girl Scouts, Boys Scouts, and Camp Fire Girls and Boys that stresses the philosophies of the organization.

Special Needs Camps

There are many camps for children who have disabilities or special concerns to help them meet other kids with similar disabilities, feel safe and supported, work with an experienced staff, get away from their problems, and make improvements in specific areas. Here are some of the camps available to children with special needs:

Abused, neglected, or abandoned children camp	Arthritis camp
	Asthma camp

ADHD (attention deficit hyperactivity disorder) camp

Autism camp

Burn camp

Cancer and oncology camp

Cerebral palsy camp

Chronic illness camp

Cystic fibrosis camp

Diabetes camp

Disadvantaged kids camp

Epilepsy camp

Foster children camp

Heart disease camp

Hemophilia camp

HIV/AIDS camp

Learning disabilities camp

Multiple sclerosis camp

Muscular dystrophy camp

Obesity and weight loss camp

Physical disabilities camp

Sickle cell anemia camp

Speech and hearing impairments camp

Spina bifida camp

Spinal cord injuries camp

Substance abuse camp

Visually impaired/blind camp

Sports Camps

If your child has a special interest in sports and wants to compete with others or improve his abilities, you might want to consider a sports camp. Some of the camps offer a variety of sports and games, while others specialize in a specific sport or activity. Here are some of the most common sports-related camps:

Bicycle camp

Cheerleading camp

Equestrian (horseback riding) camp

Golf camp

Gymnastics camp

Martial arts camp

Mountain climbing camp

Roller blading camp

Skateboard camp

Tennis camp

Team Sports Camps

While some camps offer individual sport skills, others offer the opportunity to participate in team sports so that kids learn competition, cooperation, and teamwork:

Basketball camp
Field hockey camp
Football camp
Soccer camp
Softball or baseball camp
Track and field camp
Volleyball camp

Travel and Trip Camps

Some camps specialize in travel opportunities, moving from place to place, often by hiking, horseback riding, or rafting. Many camps transport the necessary gear for the campers, while others encourage kids to tote their own stuff.

Water Sports Camps

Camps with water resources and activities are always popular with kids, especially during the hot summer months. Look for camps that include the following water activities:

Boating	Rowing
Canoeing	Scuba diving
Diving	Swimming
Rafting	Water skiing

Wilderness and Survival Camps

For extreme campers, you might consider a survival camp in the wilderness, where the kids must use their camping skills and information to "survive" while hiking, climbing, map-and-compass reading, and camping.

Winter Sports Camps

If your child has the opportunity to go to camp in the winter or where there are winter activities, you might find the following camps:

Ice hockey camp   Ski camp
Ice skating camp   Snowboarding camp

Where to Find Good Camps for Kids

Once you've decided to send your child to camp and you've got an idea about the type of camp you want for him, how do you go about finding the right camp? You can find most kinds of camps on the Internet, and while we don't endorse a particular camp, here are the Web site addresses for some specific camps that might be of interest to you and your child:

Ace Computer Camps: computer camp for kids;
www.computercamp.com

American Computer Camps: information and referrals;
www.acacamps.org

Association of Jewish Sponsored Camps: camp for Jewish
kids; www.jewishcamps.org

Boggy Creek Gang: camp for kids with chronic illnesses;
www.boggycreek.org

Boy Scouts of America: camp for Cub and Boy Scouts;
www.bsa.scouting.org

Camp Advisor: information and referrals;
www.campadvisor.com

Camp ASCCA: Easter Seals camp for kids with disabilities;
www.campaswcca.org

Camp Del Corazon: camp for kids with heart disease;
www.campdelcorazon.org

Campfinders: information and referrals;
www.campfinders.com

Camp Fire Girls and Boys: camp for Camp Fire kids;
www.campfire.org

Camp 4 Kids: referrals for kids with special needs;
www.camp4kids.nbc4.com

Camp Heartland: camp for kids with HIV/AIDS;
www.campheartland.org

Camp Makebelieve: camp for kids with hyperactivity disorder; www.campmakebelieve.com

CampNet: information and referrals; www.campnet.org

Camp Ronald McDonald: camp for disabled children;
www.campronaid.org

Camp Ronald McDonald for Good Times: camp for kids
with cancer; www.campronaldmcdonald.org

CampSearch: information and referrals;
www.campsearch.com

Camp Winnarainbow: circus and performing camp for
kids; www.campwinnarainbow.org

Camp Winston: camp for kids with learning disabilities
and Tourette's syndrome; www.campwinston.com

Christian Camping International: Christian camp referrals; www.gospelcom.net

Easter Seals: camp funding for special needs kids;
www.easter-seals.org

Excel Interactive Science Museum: educational camp for
kids; www.excel.org

Florida's Gulfarium: marine camp for kids;
www.gulfarium.com

Girl Scouts of USA: camp for Brownies and Girl Scouts;
www.girlscouts.org

InterCamp: information and referrals;
www.intercamp.org

KidsCamp: information and referrals;
www.kidscamp.com

Kids Golf: golf camp for kids; www.kidsgolf.com

Kids on the Net: computer camp for kids;
www.nunanet.com

Mad Science: interactive science camp for kids;
www.madscience.com

National Camp Association: information and referrals;
www.summercamp.org

Science Adventures: science camp for kids;
www.scienceadventures.com

Super Camp Guide: information and referrals;
  www.family.go.com
Trails Wilderness School: wilderness adventures in the
  West; www.trailsws.com
United Way of America: camp funding for special needs
  kids; www.unitedway.org
YMCA of the USA: Y-sponsored camps; www.ymca.net
YWCA of the USA: Y-sponsored camps; www.ywca.org

Other Ways to Find a Good Camp

While the Internet certainly provides a vast list of camp opportunities, there are other, and perhaps better, ways to find the right camp for your child.

Friends. One of the best ways to locate a good camp is to get a personal endorsement from a friend who's been to the camp. This way, you can find out what they liked about the camp firsthand and ask specific questions about the facilities, activities, staff, and food.

Recreation Center. Your local recreation center often provides camp experiences for children in the community, so check it out and see what it has to offer your child. The cost can be reasonable, and you may have the option of day camp or overnight camp.

School. Sometimes your local school offers kids an opportunity to go to camp. This way, your child can attend camp with his friends and return every year if it's a positive experience.

Church. Your local church, temple, or synagogue may have camping opportunities for children, with or without a religious slant, so ask about the options to see whether they might be what you want for your child.

Colleges and Universities. You may want to send your child to a nearby college or university for his camp experience and possibly join him with the rest of the family for a togetherness camp.

Clubs. Many charitable organizations offer camp opportunities for kids, such as Rotary, Kiwanis, YMCA, YWCA, Lions, United Way, 4-H, and so on. They're especially helpful if your child has special needs, so investigate these clubs for camp information.

Newspapers and Kids' Magazines. Many camps advertise in newspapers and kids' magazines, so you might look into some of them. Be sure to find out everything you can about the camp before you commit since you may not have any kind of endorsement about the place.

Camp Fairs. Check www.acacamps.org for a list of camp fairs that are held around the country. You'll find hands-on information about all kinds of camps, which is an excellent way to get a feeling for the various places and programs.

What You Need to Know After You've Found Your Camp

Some of the things you'll want to know about the camp you've selected are listed in the following. Go over the checklist to see how your choices compare.

What About Accreditation?

Not all camps are accredited, so you might want to find out whether your camp has achieved accreditation by the American Camping Association (ACA). The ACA makes sure that the camp meets more than 300 nationally recognized standards, including certain health and safety standards and a strict code of practices. The camp director's background is checked, as are the staff and medical personnel. And the camp is reviewed by peers and observed every three years by professionals.

Here's some information on ACA accreditation you may find useful:

◆ Accreditation is voluntary—only 30 percent of the 8,500 camps available seek accreditation.

"The best thing is opening up your suitcase on the second morning of camp and finding the shirt you planned to wear laced with candy bars and a little love note from mom."
                                              —Sue W.

- Accreditation offers the best evidence for a safe and nurturing environment.
- Accreditation means that the camp practices have been measured at national standards and go beyond basic licensing requirements of states.
- Accreditation, which is continually updated by the ACA, provides educational training, guidelines, programs, and publications for directors and staff.
- The 300 standards are overseen by trained professionals every three years.
- The ACA works with the Academy of Pediatrics, the American Red Cross, and other youth agencies to ensure the best-quality care.
- Accreditation offers programs to prevent illness and injury and to deal with crisis and emergencies.
- Accreditation provides a supervised, positive environment, with controlled boundaries to help children grow.
- Monitored areas of accreditation include site, food service, transportation, health care, management, safety regulations, staff training, staff qualifications and supervision, and program goals.

ACA's Additional Standards

Here are some of the ACA's standards that are required of approved camps:

- The camp must provide a specific ratio of campers to counselors so that quality supervision is ensured.

- The staff is trained in positive behavior management and modification to help with a child's inappropriate behavior.
- Strict policies on access to firearms and ammunition are provided to deter unsupervised use.
- Staff are trained in risk management in order to identify and control areas exposed to dangers.
- Emergency and sensitivity training is provided for all the staff.
- Campers are protected in public places or when in contact with the public.
- Security concerns are reviewed, identified, and corrected as needed.
- Regulations are provided for dealing with possible intrusion of unauthorized personnel.
- The camp offers a system for monitoring camper behavior.

Safety Concerns

The ACA advocates safety at camps and strives to make sure that all children are safe at all times. Safety measures include the following:

- Screening the staff and doing background checks
- Educating the staff on child abuse, behavior management, nighttime supervision, safety regulations, and emergency procedures
- Observing the staff while on duty and providing performance guidelines

- Supervising transportation and maintenance of vehicle safety
- Providing guidelines and supervision for water sports, including pools, lakes, canoeing, sailing, boating, and so on
- Complying with 300 standards for health, safety, and program quality before being accredited
- Reviewing camps at regular intervals to ensure compliance

What to Ask the Camp Director

Here are some questions you might want to ask the camp's director while investigating a possible camp:

- What is the camp director's philosophy? Do your goals and beliefs of discipline and child rearing match his?
- What is the camp director's background? Has he been educated in the area of child development, and has he worked extensively with children?
- Does the camp director have references? Can you contact them to find out more information?
- How does the camp director hire the staff? What qualities does he look for in his counselors and other staff members?
- How does the camp director train the staff? What kind of education and training does he provide for his staff?
- How does the camp director handle problems? If your child should have a problem with homesickness, fears, or another camper, how would he handle the situation?

When to Apply for Camp

Once you've made your final decision and have chosen the perfect camp for your child, when should you apply to ensure that your child finds a place at the camp? According to the ACA, the popularity of summer camps is increasing, with enrollment currently 10 percent higher now than 10 years ago. In fact, most campers sign up for the following year's session at the end of the previous session. So it's important to register as early as January or February for the upcoming summer session, or your child may be out of luck. Many camps offer incentives for early registrations, which makes it an even better reason to sign up soon and avoid the rush.

2

Countdown to Camp

Preparing Your Child Emotionally for the Adventure

You've chosen the best camp for your child, and you're both excited about the upcoming adventure. All you have left to do is pack some bags and wave good-bye, right? Not quite. The fantasy of going to camp isn't always the same as the reality of camp, and as the departure day approaches, your child may start to show signs of anxiety. It's easy to picture all the fun of camp, but imagining the separation, loneliness, and apprehension isn't such a pretty picture. Fortunately, there are lots of ways you can prepare your child—and yourself—for his trip away from home.

What the Camp Experience Offers Your Child

To best prepare your child for the experience, keep in mind that going to camp is a learning experience—a rite of passage that provides many opportunities for growth, independence, and self-esteem. The anxiety stems from the unknown. Your child may not have been to camp before or had any experience like it. Fear of the unknown is the major contributing cause of anxiety and homesickness.

Your child may not be the only one experiencing some anxiety. Many parents also worry about the separation. You may be concerned that your child will be unhappy, won't fit in, will suffer from homesickness, and won't make new friends. Deep down you may believe she won't last through the experience and will want to come home.

These feelings are normal. Acknowledging them is the first step toward coping with them. Talk to your child about her feelings of camp and share your own feelings as you discuss the adventure ahead. Here are some topics you might want to include in your discussion of the impending departure to camp.

Going to Camp Is a Learning Experience

Your child is going to learn all kinds of new skills, new information, and new ways of thinking, so stress this when you talk about camp. He'll learn social skills, such as how to make new friends, how to get along with others, and how to survive without his parents. He'll learn cognitive skills, such as how to solve problems that arise, how to cope when the problems can't be solved, and how to share his problems with those in authority. Finally, he'll learn physical skills, such as how to swim, hike, play group games, increase his stamina, and challenge his growing body.

Separation from Parents Is a Personal Growth Experience

Being away from the supervision and guidance of parents for a week or more helps a child realize she has the skills to be an independent, self-sufficient, and productive person. Separation from parents allows a child to be more aware of herself, her abilities, her attitudes, and her feelings. She's given the opportunity to make her own decisions, think for herself, and discover that she can survive on her own in a safe and supervised place.

Being at Camp Offers Your Child a Safe and Structured Environment

This new setting gives your child the chance to explore new opportunities, skills, friendships, and challenges. He'll learn to work with other adults who have been educated and trained in the area of child development, and he'll discover that he can trust other adults besides his parents. He'll realize that there are other people who care about him, believe in him, and want to help him be the best he can be.

Being on Her Own Helps a Child Become More Confident in Herself and Her Abilities

She'll enjoy her successes and deal with her failures as she becomes more competent and able to succeed. As her sense of self develops, her self-esteem will rise, and she'll learn to master new skills and cope with problems. Self-confidence comes from trying new things and succeeding—or dealing with failure—and is important for your child's all-around growth.

How to Prepare for Camp Together

Here are some specific ways for you and your child to get ready for camp.

Prepare Together

You've worked together to find the right camp, so keep that collaboration going. Involve your child in the preparations so that he feels a part of the whole experience and more in control of his own adventure. Let him study the brochures, check

"Send along a family picture to help your child deal with homesickness. Hide it in a book if your child is apt to feel embarrassed by having the picture in front of his friends."
—Charu B.

off what he likes, and make lists of the things he wants to take to camp and what he wants to do when he gets there.

Let Her Choose

When you investigate the various camps, compare several choices and discuss the pros and cons of each one with your child. Let her know why you like some camps over others, but try to allow her the opportunity to contribute to the final decision. If you have an objection to her choice, explain your reason to her clearly so she'll understand why she needs to make another selection.

Check Out the Camp

If at all possible, send for brochures and ask for a video that shows the details of the camp, or check out the place on the Internet. Even better, make a visit to camp so your child can see what's ahead. This will help relieve much of his anxiety— and yours.

Talk to the Director

The camp director should be accessible to both of you, so take the time to talk with him, ask questions (see chapter 1 for a list), and then let your child have a chat with the director, too, so she's a part of the process and comfortable with her choice. If your child is a bit shy on the phone, ask the director whether he has e-mail and let your child send her questions via electronic messages.

Pack Together

Several weeks before it's time to go to camp, make a list of all the things your child might want to take. (See chapter 3 for suggestions.) Discuss each item, why it's needed, or why it might not be appropriate for camp. Then when it's nearly time to go to camp, pack the bags as a team so he knows what's available to him and what everything is for.

Talk About Camp

Take time to share your stories about your camp experiences and what your child can expect. Let her know about the fun you had and how you solved your own problems as they arose. Have a sense of humor about some of the sticky situations you experienced to show her how you can laugh about some problems after they're over. Give her lots of encouragement and let her know you believe in her, but don't overdo the praise, or it will sound empty.

Share Your Feelings

Don't ignore your child's feelings of anxiety or fears of going to camp. These feelings are real and need to be acknowledged and discussed. After your child has expressed his feelings and concerns, talk them over and show him ways of coping with them. Share your own feelings, too, and be realistic about the good and the bad, but don't go overboard on the negatives and cause even more anxiety in your child. Keep a positive attitude and share your confidence in your child as you talk about the adventures of camp.

Remember to Have Fun!

The purpose of camp is to have a great time—and for the most part your child will do just that. If problems arise, they can be solved or dealt with, and there are plenty of caring adults there to assist her. Just remind her of all the benefits of camp:

- Making new friends
- Experiencing a new environment
- Getting a break from routine
- Gaining independence
- Challenging yourself

Here are even more ways both parents and kids benefit from the camp experience:

- Parents get a vacation from their children so they're refreshed.
- Child takes a break from television and video games.
- Child gets time off from problems in his life.
- Child is exposed to an environment different from his own.
- Child learns about cultural differences.
- Child finds out about nature and the out-of-doors.
- Child gets a chance to practice letting go.
- Child learns teamwork and how to develop better social skills.
- Child has the opportunity to explore his creativity.
- Child challenges himself physically and intellectually.
- Child gets to get dirty and be himself.
- Child learns to believe in himself.

- Child discovers he can survive.
- Parents realize they can survive without child for a short time.

Have a "Camp Video Night"

One fun way to prepare for camp is to spend an evening or two watching camp-related videos over a bowl of popcorn. You can laugh at the humor, discuss some of the problems that arise, and talk about ways you would solve a situation if you were there. Here are some recommendations for videos you should be able to find at the video store, along with their ratings:

Addams Family Values (PG-13): The kids from the creepy family go to camp and make friends.

Camp Nowhere (PG): Kids take over a defunct camp.

Ernest Goes to Camp (PG): Goofy Ernest wants to be a camp counselor.

Heavyweights (PG): Overweight kids are forced to go to camp and end up having a good time.

Meatballs (PG): Bill Murray takes over camp as a crazy counselor.

Parent Trap (Hayley Mills version, G; new version, PG-13): Two versions about separated twins who meet at camp and scheme to get their parents back together.

Race for Your Life, Charlie Brown (G): The Peanuts gang goes to camp.

Space Camp (PG): Five teens go to Space Camp, then get caught on a shuttle.

How to Deal with Homesickness

Most kids wouldn't have second thoughts about going to camp if it weren't for homesickness. It's the thought of separation from parents, missing friends, and being away from home and their own bedrooms that keep some children from even trying camp. Homesickness is normal in kids—millions of children experience it when they go to camp. In fact, if they didn't miss the security of their family, they wouldn't be typical. But kids are resilient, and most of them can cope with homesickness if it's understood, discussed, and dealt with.

Homesickness Is Normal

The majority of children—more than 80 to 90 percent—experience some degree of homesickness when they go to camp. When a child says he's homesick, it means he misses his home, family, friends, and pets. Some kids even miss home cooking, their favorite television shows, their toys, and a number of other things, so it's often different for everyone. But when a child experiences homesickness, it also means he has something wonderful to look forward to at the end of camp—coming home again! (See chapter 4 for ideas on making the homecoming extra special.) Kids often appreciate home much more after they return from camp.

Only 1 percent of children who go to camp experience such severe homesickness that they return home early, so the odds are your child will make it through the session. Here are some ways to help your child prepare for and deal with the possibility of homesickness while away at camp.

Preparing Your Child for the Separation

There are lots of ways to help your child prepare for going away to camp. Each child is unique, so different techniques work for different kids. Try a variety of the following tips, and you'll probably have a successful separation. At the same time, be patient and understanding and let her express her feelings and concerns about leaving home.

Let your child make some decisions. Be sure to get your child involved in choosing the camp so he feels like he's a part of the process. The more control he has over his choices, the more independent he'll feel, which helps him deal with feelings of loneliness and homesickness.

Create a countdown calendar. Several weeks before it's time to go to camp, make a countdown calendar. Photocopy the weeks or months your child will be away. Then mark the opening day, the end of camp, and all the special events that will occur during the session (an activity list is often provided by the camp ahead of time). For example, you might include the following: "First Day of Camp!" "Last Day of Camp!," "Fourth of July," "Your Birthday," "Water Skiing Day," "Camp Talent Show," and so on. This way your child will have lots to look forward to each day. If the camp doesn't provide an activity list, make up some special days, such as "National Giggling Day," "Trick-a-Counselor Day," or "Make a Nature Collage Day."

Do some role playing. Get involved in some make-believe and try out different scenarios that might occur at camp so that your child can see how he might react in different situations. You might act out making new friends, talking to a counselor about a problem, or dealing with a bear.

Practice camping. Head for the backyard or local campground and spend a night or two under the stars and among nature. Let your child get a feeling for what it's like to go camping and how much fun it can be. Give her lots of things to do while at camp to help him feel competent and independent. After the experience is over, ask your child what she liked the most and what she'd like to do next time. If you've done plenty of camping as a family, have your child invite a friend or two to spend the night in the backyard all by themselves.

Have fun in the dark. If your child is afraid of the dark, give him a flashlight and lots of batteries to store in his sleeping bag for security and comfort. Then play some nighttime games to keep him occupied at night until he becomes drowsy and falls asleep. We've got some games in chapter 3 you might want to practice together ahead of time.

"Send a family scrapbook you make ahead of time. Have each family member create his or her own page, with a picture of themselves, a note, a drawing, or a game. Write pages for the family pets too, then tuck it in the suitcase to discover at camp." —*Priscilla H.*

Visit the camp. If at all possible, visit the camp so your child gets a feeling for the place and feels comfortable about going there. If you can't visit, ask the camp to send a video or brochure about the place and visit the Web site if there is one. Then have her talk to the director or send him an e-mail.

Invite a friend. If your child is really reluctant to go to camp by himself, see whether he has a friend or sibling who might want to join him. He may feel more secure if there's one other familiar face at the camp.

Talk about it. Remember, talking about being homesick doesn't create homesickness. You're just acknowledging the feelings that are there. Remind your child that sometimes new experiences are difficult or even painful but that something good always comes from a learning experience and that she'll feel good about her accomplishment. Tell her the time will go by before she knows it, and soon she'll be back home again. Assure her that in a day or two, she'll be over her homesickness. In fact, when she returns home, she may even be homesick for camp!

Coping with Homesickness While He's Away at Camp

Here are some ways to help your child deal with homesickness after he's left for camp.

Pack some fun. Tuck away a few small games and some activity books to keep him busy when he's alone or between activities at camp. Travel games are prefect for this, and so are puzzles, joke books, and kids' books. If your child is kept occupied, he's not as likely to feel homesick.

Include an old favorite. Find something special that belongs to your child and include it in the suitcase, such as a favorite T-shirt, a stuffed animal, a special photograph, a raggedy old robe, and so on. This will help her feel more comfortable and secure at camp.

Keep in touch. If you can arrange phone calls ahead of time, set some specific times for your conversations. Give your child a prepaid calling card so he has easy access to the phone. Be advised that sometimes phone calls can backfire and might make a child feel even more homesick, so be sure to discuss this with the camp counselor.

Send care packages. Every few days you might want to pack up some goodies and send them along to camp. A new comic book, some trail mix, a pack of gum, pictures from home, silly toys, joke books, and other small items really give kids a lift when they're away.

Provide a journal. Stuff a small blank journal into the suitcase, along with a fun pen, and encourage your child to write about her experiences each day. If she puts her thoughts on paper, it will occupy her time and give her a chance to express herself, and she'll have something to help her remember all the fun she had when she gets home.

What *Not* to Do

Here are a few tips on what not to do about homesickness:

- Don't overstate how much you'll miss your child. Let him know you care, but tell him you'll also be glad to see him when he returns and that you're proud of him for going.
- Don't bribe her into going to camp. The reward she receives is the pride she feels in herself, and no toy, game, or pet can substitute for that sense of accomplishment.
- Don't talk up camp too much or promise things the camp may not deliver since the experience might not live up to your description. He may end up feeling disappointed with camp and may not trust you the next time you promise something that doesn't materialize.
- Don't feel guilty about sending your child to camp. She's going to be gone only a short time, and she'll return home a better person, so you're doing a good thing for her. You're also allowed to enjoy the peace and quiet while she's gone!
- Don't take your child's venting too seriously. He may let out all his feelings to you, but as soon as he's finished, he'll probably feel better. Just listen to him, understand his feelings, and encourage him to continue with his plans.

- Don't hesitate to talk with the camp director if you're really concerned. You may want to discuss your child's fears ahead of time with the director and see what he recommends for homesickness. Let your child talk to the director, too, and ask any questions she might have that will help allay her fears.
- Don't succumb too early to your child's cries for home. The number of children who suffer from severe homesickness is extremely small, so give your child a second chance to succeed before "rescuing" him.
- Don't make your child feel like a failure if she decides to come home after all. Focus on her successes—how many days she made it and what she accomplished—and talk about trying camp again next year.

Signs That Your Child Might Be Severely Homesick

If you suspect your child is really having a hard time at camp, in spite of everything you've done to help him, you may want to collect him early. As stated earlier, only about 1 percent of children quit camp in the middle of the session, but for them homesickness is a real and debilitating fear, and to remain at camp feeling terrified, abandoned, or alone may be more traumatizing than forcing him to stay. Watch for the following signs that your child's homesickness is serious:

- If she threatens to run away from camp and go home on her own
- If he threatens to harm himself

- If she has trouble making new friends or avoids socializing with others
- If he doesn't participate in any of the activities or events
- If the child is acting in a destructive or disruptive way that interferes with the activities of camp
- If she is extremely anxious, severely depressed, sad or crying, or withdrawn or lethargic or has other symptoms of depression
- If he doesn't eat or sleep for two days

The camp counselors and directors are trained to recognize signs of depression in children and should contact you if the homesickness cannot be easily overcome in a couple of days. If you have to retrieve your child early, try not to make him feel like a failure. Let him talk out his feelings, then find a way to help raise his self-esteem in other ways to make up for the negative experience.

Mail Call: Keeping in Touch with Your Child

The best way to help your child make a smooth transition to camp is to keep in touch through personal letters and special

"Send along something, such as ribbons or bandannas, for all the kids in your child's cabin or tent so they all feel special." —*Vanessa H.*

packages while she's away. If you prepare ahead of time, your child won't miss a minute of contact with the family and will know she's missed and loved even though she's away from home. And all children love to get mail from home! Here are some fun ways to keep in touch with your child while she's on her own.

Mail Early

Plan to send a few letters to the camp even before your child leaves home so that the notes, messages, and packages are waiting for him when he arrives. He'll be surprised and delighted to receive these special letters the first day. Then keep those cards and letters coming. There's nothing better than getting mail from home while you're at camp.

Make It Fun

Instead of writing boring letters on plain paper and mailing them in ordinary envelopes, jazz up your correspondence with decorative papers, colored inks, and wild envelopes. There are lots of fun papers today—decorated with balloons, cats, cartoon characters, and holiday designs—available at stationery, office supply, and copy stores. These festive papers make receiving information from home a lot more inviting. Use puffy pens, glitter pens, and colored inks to write your message and try different styles of handwriting, such as bubble letters, shaded letters, curly letters, and so on, when you pen your note. Finally, decorate the envelope with stickers, designs, and bright colors and address the envelope to your child using decorative letters. See how creative you can be with your letters and envelopes for fun.

Special Surprises

Slip something special inside the letter as a surprise bonus each time you post it. Think about what kinds of flat items you can include, such as sticks of gum, trading cards, photographs, comic strips, puzzle pages, notepads, miniature books, hair ribbons, wild socks, and so on. You can add silly stuff, too, such as a goofy picture of the family, a pair of your kid's underwear, an old toy, some lawn cuttings, and so on, for an extra laugh.

Hidden Notes

Another fun way to keep in contact with your child is to hide little notes in her suitcase that she'll find at different times throughout her camp session. For example, you might write a simple message, such as "We think you're great!" or "Don't forget to wash your socks!" and tuck them

into a suitcase compartment or a pair of folded socks. Fill her pants pockets, soap holder, sneakers, purse, or even the inside of her hat with notes, jokes, or silly poems. She'll never know when another one will turn up to surprise her.

Address Book

Include an address book filled with addresses for all your child's friends and family. While he's at camp, he can add the addresses of his new friends he's met during the session. Don't forget to give him some fun stationery and pre-addressed stamped envelopes to make it easy.

Be Silly

Once in a while, write a silly letter signed by your child's toys, baby sister or brother, or even the family pets! Here's one to get you started:

Dear Camp Kid:

The Cat and I miss you.

Since you've been gone, we've been sleeping in your bed!

We also ate all your favorite cereals—Cat Crunchies and Puppy Puffs.

And now we get to watch our favorite TV shows—Real Dog World and Cat From Planet Furball.

Your parents are taking us to Disneyland, too! I get to meet Pluto.

Hope you're having fun at camp. We're having fun turning your room into an Animal Retreat.

Say hi to the camp squirrels for us. And bring us back some nature toys.

Signed, Fluffy the Cat and Drooler the Dog

Letter Prompts

If your child isn't much of a letter writer, get him started with some letter prompts or fill-in-the-blanks. Prepare the letters ahead of time—one for each day of camp—and fill in your own name, address, and the date. Start the letter with an opening line or greeting, then leave the rest blank for your child to fill in with camp news. Then address enough envelopes to go with the letters, stamp them, and they'll be ready to go as soon as your child fills them in.

Here's a sample letter that might give you ideas for your own letter prompts. You might also make prompts for other family members and friends, including sister or brother, grandparents, or even the family pets!

Dear Mom and Dad:

I like camp because _____ .

I am doing a lot of _____ .

The food here tastes like _____ .

I've met some new friends named _____ and

_____ .

My favorite thing to do is _____ .

I can't wait to _____ !

See you in _____ days.

Love, _____

3

Packin' Up

What to Pack for Camp and Send Along for Fun

Your child may be so excited about camp, he'll want to pack his bag the moment he's signed up. Let him have fun with his suitcase—you can always repack for real when it's time to go. In the meantime, make a list of the things you think he'll need or want while he's away and ask him to make a list, too. When it's time, have your child pack the bag with you so that he knows what's inside and can add a few things he thinks are absolutely necessary.

What Your Child Needs to Take

We've done most of the decision making for you in this section. Here's our list of all the things you might want to pack—and some of the things you *don't* need to send.

Bedding

Your child will probably need some kind of bedding, unless the camp provides everything, which is rare. Send along a warm sleeping bag or sheets and blankets if there's already a mattress. Even in summer, nighttimes are often cold at camp locales, and you don't want your camper to be uncomfortably chilly.

Pillow

Don't forget to pack your child's pillow. Most camps don't offer pillows, and if they do, they're pretty uncomfortable. Send the one she's used to—her own personal pillow. It will help her get to sleep at night and make her feel more secure. If the pillowcase is decorated with cartoon figures or designs, ask whether she wants to take that one or substitute a plain white case instead (so she doesn't get teased).

Towels

Don't send your best towels since you probably won't get them back the same way you sent them. Pick out some towels you don't care about. Your child isn't likely to care what they look like, either. Pack a variety of sizes—washcloth, hand towel, bath towel, and beach towel—to provide for all his needs. Towels are versatile and are often used for many things besides just drying off from showers and swimming.

Toiletries

Have your child help you pick out the toiletries, such as the following suggested items, depending on his or her needs:

Soap
Face care items
Shampoo and crème rinse
Toothpaste, floss, and
    toothbrush
Comb and brush

Deodorant
Hair products
Makeup
Nail clippers
Personal hygiene products
    (sanitary pads, tampons,
    etc.)

Toiletries Bag

Include a small, sturdy plastic bag to store and carry toiletries that travel back and forth between the tent and latrine.

Clothes

Even though there's a good chance your child may wear the same outfit every single day while at camp, pack a variety of clothes for different weather, activities, and comfort. Most camps provide a list of clothing items required, but in case they don't, here are some of the basics:

Two pairs of shorts
Two or three T-shirts, long sleeved and short sleeved
Two or three pairs of jeans or long pants
Durable, comfortable shoes
Hiking boots
Athletic shoes
Flip-flops
Hat for sun protection
Raincoat or poncho for rain
Warm jacket for cold
Bathing suit and cover-up

Laundry Pen

Use a permanent black marker or laundry pen to mark *everything* with your child's name—*everything*.

"Make sure you always bring some form of candy to camp. This can be used for a number of things. Bribery—if you don't want to clean up your bunk, you can pay someone with candy to do it for you. Pranks—hide a piece of candy somewhere in another camper's tent and in a few hours there will be an anthill camped out in that tent." —*Josh L.*

Laundry Bag, Duffel Bag, Carry Bag, or Pillowcase

Use the bag to store dirty clothes and to transport the clothes to the laundry area. Remind him not to store his clean clothes in the dirty laundry bag.

Laundry Products

You probably won't find a laundry service at the camp, but there may be washing and drying facilities the kids can use if they're going to be there longer than one to two weeks. Include small packs of detergent in the suitcase and some coins, if they're required.

First Aid Supplies

Pack first aid products in a separate container that your child can retrieve and access quickly if necessary. Make it portable enough so that she can take it with her on hikes and outings, too. Here are some of the things you should include in your first aid kit:

Bug and tick repellent
Sunscreen
Lip balm
Water bottle or canteen
Band-Aids or bandages and tape
Facial tissues or wet wipes

Antibacterial cream or spray

Whistle (in case your child is in danger, he can blow the
whistle for help)

Tweezers (to take out simple splinters)

Medication (send your child's medications in their origi-
nal bottles with the dosage clearly marked, along with
any medical release forms required; make sure the
medical staff knows about the medications for your
child)

Required Forms

Most camps will want insurance forms, health forms, and
other paperwork necessary for the protection of your child
and the camp. Send any other forms you think your child will
need to provide.

Additional Equipment

Here are some additional supplies to consider.

Flashlight

Batteries

Disposable camera

Canteen or water bottle

Compass

Mess kit

Collapsible cup

Survival guide

What You Might Want to Include

Although not absolutely necessary, here are some things that might be nice to have—if you can fit them into the suitcase.

Spending Money

There may be a store, trading post, or canteen where your child can buy treats, souvenirs, or other items, so you might want to include a little extra money. Check with the camp to make sure this is allowed, and don't send a lot of money that may be lost or stolen.

Bandanna

A simple bandanna can come in handy in a dozen ways—to tie back hair, to use as a sweatband, to carry small or delicate items, to sit on, to use for cleanup, to wave at others for attention, to wrap injuries, and so on.

Spray Bottle with Fan

If your child is going to a camp where it's likely to be very warm, tuck one of those spray bottles that come with a fan into his suitcase to keep him cool and refreshed.

Soap on a Rope

Poke a hole in the middle of a bar of soap with a nail, then slip a two-foot-long cord through the hole and tie it off. When your child gets to camp, she can hang the soap on a tree or a hook in the latrine for quick and easy use.

Hair Dryer

Many kids have come to rely on the hair dryer to fix their hair, so include a mini-dryer if you have space in the suitcase and the camp allows it. Make sure the latrine has electricity, and go over safety rules for using the dryer and other electrical appliances around water.

Extra Pillowcase

Your child will need one pillowcase to cover the pillow, but it's nice to have an extra to store laundry and carry stuff. He can also stuff it with extra clothes for more comfort at bedtime. And get it autographed by all the campers on the last day of camp.

Small Backpack

Provide a small backpack for short hiking trips to store items your child will want to take along.

Camp Book

Send along this book and others that might come in handy during the camp experience. Books about nature, animals, and the area where your child will be staying will help enrich the adventure.

Oversized White T-Shirts

Your child can use a big shirt as a cover-up, to sleep in, and to decorate with her friends on the last day of camp.

Colored Pens

Include some fabric pens, permanent felt pens, puffy pens, or other markers to decorate T-shirts, pillowcases, and other arts and crafts items.

Autograph/Address Book

Give your camper an autograph book and an address book so he can collect signatures and addresses of his new friends and write to them when camp is over.

Scrunchies or Hair Bands

It's nice to have some kind of hair band if your child has long hair to keep it out of the way when it's hot outside, the hair is long, or it gets wet.

Tank Tops

Tank tops are great for keeping cool and comfortable on a hot day.

Camp Vest

Buy a camp vest with lots of pockets so your child can store small items and carry them while hiking, boating, or playing.

Tip

A large zip lock plastic bag filled with air or a large piece of foam can serve as a pillow.

Awesome Shirt

Send along your child's favorite T-shirt that features a movie star, rock singer, interesting saying, or cartoon. It makes a great conversation piece, and if it's his favorite, it'll make him feel better.

Bathrobe

Send a bathrobe in case your child's pajamas are a little ragged or skimpy or it's cold outside during that long trek to the latrine in the middle of the night.

Shower Shoes or Flip-Flops

Include shower shoes or flip-flops so your child doesn't have to stand in dirty shower water. They're also great for walking on hot or rough sandy beaches or rocks.

Things You Don't Need to Pack

Here are some of the things most camps discourage, so think twice before you allow your child to take them along:

Radio, boom box, or CD player
Portable television
Video games
Cell phones, pagers
Food (that might attract ants or bears)
Knives (unless permitted)
Fireworks
Expensive or fancy clothes or jewelry

Boredom Busters: Fun Things to Send Along

One of the main causes of homesickness is boredom. When a child doesn't have enough to keep her engaged or occupied, she begins to think about home, family, friends, and everything she misses. But if you keep her stimulated and busy, she's more likely to stay in the moment and forget about home, at least temporarily. Here are some suggestions for keeping your child busy—and happy—at camp.

Games

Pack some favorite box games or travel games, such as Monopoly, Careers, Yahtzee, Dominoes, or Clue, to play with other kids. Buy the travel size—they're smaller and fit more easily into the suitcase. Add some games your child can play alone, too, such as Bop-It, Simon, Solitaire, or Jacks, in case his new friends are busy.

Activities

Give your child some activities to occupy her time when camp is quiet, such as colored markers, construction paper, scissors and glue, embroidery floss, fabric or puffy paints, stickers, and beads. Arts and crafts supplies can help your child make something fun for other kids, too, while she uses her creativity and imagination.

Jokes

Pick up an inexpensive paperback joke book for kids from the bookstore or library and give your child the opportunity to entertain himself or others with a few laughs. He'll be the hit of the campsite with his humor and turn the campers into a bunch of giggling goofballs.

Magic

Visit your local toy store or magic store and buy some simple but surprising magic tricks to send to camp. You'll find old favorites, such as the "Disappearing Coin Trick," "Endless Scarf Trick," and "Rabbit in a Hat Trick," as well as lots of new ones. You can also pick up a book of simple magic tricks for your child to study and learn before he goes to camp. Then he can astound—and teach—his new friends a few tricks.

Hobbies and Collections

Talk with your child about what kind of collection she might want to start while at camp, such as rocks and gems, leaves and flowers, insects, nature photographs, gum wrappers, camp song lyrics, and so on. Give her a scrapbook or box to keep her collection in and a journal or record book to make notes.

Puzzles, Mazes, and Quizzes

Include puzzle books or miniature puzzles to play with when there's time. Add maze books and fun quizzes to challenge him during breaks. If you have time, make up your own puzzles and quizzes to entertain your child for added fun, such as "Family Trivia," "Camp Questions," or even "Worst Case Scenarios."

Cards and Card-Playing Handbook

Don't forget a deck of cards—they're small, easy to carry, and offer all sorts of time-filling entertainment. To make the cards even more fun, include a small handbook that explains a variety of different card games the kids can play. Learn a few games before your child goes and let her learn a few on her own when she gets to camp.

Scrapbook and Journal

Pack a do-it-yourself scrapbook your child can fill with mementos while he's at camp. He might want to include postcards from home, leaves from camp, photos of new friends, and daily camp activity flyers. Encourage him to write in his journal each day about his experiences, his new friends, his feelings, his thoughts, and things he's learned while at camp. Don't forget tape or glue and colored markers so he can complete the book before he arrives home.

Surprises to Pack for Added Fun

When you're finished packing the bag, sneak into it just before your child is about to leave and slip in a few surprises to greet him at camp when he opens up his suitcase, such as the following:

Travel Games

Include some puzzles, cards, and other fun things to do at camp in case she gets bored or is lonely. Portable games are also a great way to attract new friends.

Trail Mix

Stir up some goodies to snack on when the cafeteria is closed and seal them in an airtight container to keep the bugs and bears away (see recipes later in this chapter, beginning on page 69).

Magazines and Books

When your child has some downtime, he'll want something quiet to do. Kids' and teen magazines are perfect for this, as are favorite comic books, camp-related novels (see the list later in this chapter), nature books, and miniature books.

Lovey

Slip your child's lovey, teddy bear, old blanket, or other special item that offers her a feeling of security and reminder of home. Make sure it's well hidden so the other kids don't see it, in case they're apt to tease her.

If Your Child Forgets Something

No matter how well you plan, you almost always forget something. If it's important, such as medication, you can mail it for next-day delivery. You might also call the camp director and see whether there's some way the item can be substituted to save you the trouble and expense of mailing it. Finally, if it's really not that important, let your child figure out a way to cope without it and make do with what he has. This provides him with another learning opportunity—part of the reason he's at camp.

Books to Send Along

One of the best things you can send along to camp with your child is a book. When she has some time to relax or feels lonely or can't get to sleep at night, she can pick up one of the books you've packed away and escape into another world through reading. Think about what kinds of books your child likes, such as adventures, mysteries, romances, nonfiction, and so on, and then include some in the suitcase as a surprise. Even kids who don't read much may get hooked on reading while at camp. Here are some camp-related books that might be fun for your child while she's away from home.

Camp-Themed Books

Pick up some of the following books at the library or bookstore and share them with your child to help prepare him for camp. We've noted the reading level as follows: "easy" (for beginning readers) and "middle" (for middle-grade readers).

Camp Nowhere by R. L. Stine (middle): After being teased, Russell is going to prove how brave he is at the haunted falls.

Camp-Out Mystery: Boxcar Children by Gertrude Warner
(middle): Kids want to relax at camp but stumble on
a mystery—things are disappearing from the tent.

*Case of the Cheerleading Camp Mystery: A Mary-Kate and Ashley
Adventure* by Lisa Fiedler (middle): Ashley's pompoms
disappear at camp, so the twins try to find out where
they went and why.

Case of the Dog Camp Mystery: A Mary-Kate and Ashley Adventure by Judy Katschke (easy): The twins go to camp for
dogs—and the dogs disappear.

Case of the Haunted Camp by Nina Alexander (easy): Camp
is haunted, but the twins don't believe it until something strange happens.

Case of the Haunted Camp: Sweet Valley Kids by Francine Pas-
cal (easy): Someone destroys the art room at camp, so
the Super Snoopers must investigate.

Curse of Camp Cold Lake: Goosebumps by R. L. Stine (middle):
More scary stuff at camp by the horror writer.

Danny and the Dinosaur Go to Camp by Syd Hoff (easy):
Danny takes Dino to camp, where they learn new things
and especially how to help each other.

Fat Camp Commandos by Daniel Pinkwater (middle): Overweight kids get humorous revenge at camp and run away.

I Don't Want to Go to Camp by Eve Bunting (easy): A young
girl finally decides to go to camp when she learns how
fun it will be.

Kids' E-Mail and Letters from Camp by Bill Adler (middle):
A humorous collection of letters from kids at camp.

Letter from Camp by Kate Klise (middle): Brother and sister
arrive at camp, fighting, until they notice how strange

camp is. They need to stick together to solve the mystery of Camp Happy Harmony.

Lights Out! Kids Talk About Summer Camp by Eric Arnold (middle): Kids share their feelings about camp.

My Camp-Out by Marcia Leonard (middle): A young girl sleeps out in the backyard and gets frightened.

Mystery of the Haunted Caves by Penny Warner (middle): Four Girl Scouts solve a mystery at Jamboree camp in the Gold Country.

Pee Wee Scouts: Camp Ghost-Away by Judy Delton (easy): The kids hear a scary voice at camp. Everyone thinks there's a ghost—but is there?

Pinky and Rex Go to Camp by James Howe (easy): A boy worries about going to camp and ends up having a great time.

Return to Ghost Camp by R. L. Stine (middle): More scary stuff from the *Goosebumps* guy.

Snake Camp by George Stanley (easy): A boy thinks he's going to computer camp (it's called "Viper" Camp) but ends up at snake camp—and he's terrified of snakes.

Twisted Summer by Willow Davis Roberts (middle): A girl helps solve a mystery at a cabin.

"Send pictures of the family pets with funny captions underneath them, saying things like 'I'm enjoying sleeping in your bed,' or 'Hope you bring me a squirrel to play with.'"
                                                    —Colleen M.

Welcome to Camp Nightmare: Goosebumps by R. L. Stine (middle): Another scary time at camp.

Werewolves Don't Go to Summer Camp by Debbie Dadey (middle): Could hairy Mr. Jenkins really be a werewolf?

Other Packing Ideas

There are lots of ways to help make your child feel welcome, secure, and comfortable at camp, especially by helping her pack so she can personalize the environment and make it camper friendly—in a word, more like home. Here are some tips you might suggest to your child when it comes time to set up her space.

Make It Personal

When setting up camp, tell your child to organize his stuff so it's easy to access. Then suggest he make a name sign out of construction paper, tuck it into the suitcase, and hang it up to identify his space. He can bring pictures from home and other items to tack or tape up to personalize it even more. His campmates may gather around to learn more about your child from the pictures and other items—a nice way to break the ice.

Stash Your Valuables

Some kids bring money to camp to buy extra items, but if you provide extra cash, remind your child to keep it safe by stashing it away somewhere secret. Although most kids can be trusted, it's better to prevent the temptation by creating a secret compartment to store her valuables. You might roll the money into a pair of socks—dirty ones are an even better deterrent! Or tuck it into an envelope and glue the envelope to the inside of a book. You can also sew an extra secret pocket into a pair of pants by adding a square of cloth and keep the money in there. Some stores sell funny gizmos that look like drink cans or plain old rocks but are actually secret storage compartments.

Be Creative and Improvise

Some of the things you send with your child to camp can be used in several ways, with a little creativity. For example, show your child how a pillow case not only covers a pillow but also can be used as a tote bag, a laundry bag, or even an autographed memento of the experience. If he's not comfortable sleeping on the ground, suggest that he use his extra clothes to pad the ground, wrapped in a pillowcase or shirts. If he has to go to the bathroom in the middle of the night, tell him to use his flashlight to find his way and to tie pieces of string along the route so he can spot the path easily in the dark. If he needs something to sit on while hiking, tell him to pick up a sturdy stick and set it across two rocks. He can also use the stick to help him hike, to tie his food and extra clothes on, and to hang up his wet clothes to dry. If he needs a hat, show him how to fold one out of newspaper or use his T-shirt or bandanna as a wrap. If he needs a drinking cup, tell him to fold a stiff piece of paper into a cone or use concave rock. Just teach your child how to be creative, and he'll get the most out of some simple basics.

Keep Things Safe, Dry, and Away from Critters

Send along some string or rope to use for a clothesline at camp. Tell your child to hang up his wet suits and towels and hang his food up high using the rope so the animals don't get it. Show him how to string the rope between two trees or posts, or even between two tents, to play games, make a lean-to, or hang things.

Stuff to Keep Handy

Your child will want to have quick and easy access to a few things, so remind him to keep these handy:

Flashlight
Water bottle
Jacket or sweater
First aid kit
Deck of cards or puzzles
Emergency snacks

Treats for the Tent and Trail

Some camps don't allow or encourage kids to bring snacks from home, while others don't mind if parents send a few goodies in the suitcase or care package, as long as they're well protected from hungry ants and bears. If your child's camp allows homemade treats, try some of these you can prepare ahead of time and send along to keep your child from getting hungry between campfire roasts and cookouts.

Banana Chips

Slice two to three bananas into thin rounds. Spray a cookie sheet with vegetable spray and spread the banana slices in a single layer. Bake the banana chips at 150 degrees for about 2 hours, with the oven door open 1 inch. Turn the slices over and bake for another 2 hours, until the chips are firm and unbendable. Allow them to cool, then store them in a plastic bag or airtight tin.

Fruit Leather

Combine in a medium saucepan 2½ cups fruit puree, such as plum, apricot, peach, or nectarine, with 2 tablespoons honey and ½ teaspoon lemon juice. Bring the mixture to a boil, stirring as you cook. When the mixture thickens, remove from heat and cool slightly. Cover a cookie sheet with heavy-duty plastic wrap and tape it to the pan. Pour the mixture over the wrap and let it spread to about ¼ inch thick. Place the sheet in bright sunlight for two to three days until no longer tacky (bring it in at night). When the fruit is dry, roll it up in plastic wrap and store in an airtight container.

Hot Chocolate to Go

Combine 4 cups of dry powdered milk and 1 cup of presweetened chocolate mix in a bag. Shake well. At serving time, instruct your child to spoon 2 heaping tablespoons into cup, add hot water, and stir.

Nutty Fruity Balls

Chop ¼ cup walnuts, ¼ cup peanuts, and ¼ cup dried apricots and combine them in a bowl. Add ¼ cup sunflower seeds, ¼ cup raisins, ¼ cup coconut, and ¼ cup rolled oats and mix well. Add 2 tablespoons of honey and ¼ cup peanut butter and mix well again. Roll mixture into balls and place in an airtight tin.

Peanut Butter Balls

Mix ½ cup peanut butter with ¼ cup honey. Add ½ cup instant nonfat dry milk and knead mixture until you have a doughlike consistency (not too dry but not too sticky). Roll the dough into balls and place in an airtight tin.

Crunchy Trail Mix

Combine ½ cup each small cheese crackers, goldfish crackers, oyster crackers, small pretzels, Corn Chex cereal, and chopped nuts. Mix well and store in a sealable plastic bag or airtight tin.

Morning Trail Mix

Combine 1 cup favorite cereal, 1 cup raisins or other dried fruit, and 1 cup seeds or chopped nuts together in a bowl and mix well. Add 1 cup coconut and 1 cup chocolate chips if desired. Mix well and store in a sealable plastic bag or airtight tin.

Popcorn Trail Mix

Combine 1 cup chopped walnuts or peanuts, 1 cup sunflower seeds, 1 cup raisins, and 3 cups popcorn. Mix well and store in a sealable plastic bag or airtight tin.

Tropical Trail Mix

Combine 2 cups granola, ½ cup coconut, ½ cup chopped dates, and ¼ cup chopped peanuts in a sealable plastic bag and mix well. Store in bag or airtight tin.

If you don't have time to make up treats ahead of time, just tuck a few of these packaged goodies into the suitcase for your child to discover when he gets to camp. Include enough to share with others—it's a great way to make new friends!

Apples
Bag of popped popcorn
Bag of wrapped candy
Beef jerky
Breadsticks
Breakfast bars or power bars
Cheese strips or string cheese
Dried apricots or other dried fruit
Fruit roll-ups
Individually packaged cereals
Packaged cheese and crackers
Packaged fruit drinks
Peanuts, pistachios, or other nuts in the shell

Pretzels

Small crackers—goldfish, oyster, or cheese

Squirtable cheese spread

Sunflower seeds

Games to Send to Camp

Although the camp activities are likely to keep your child occupied most of the day and evening, she may find she has a few minutes of free time now and then. To prevent boredom, help her make new friends, and keep her from becoming homesick, include a few games to keep her busy and amused.

Deck of Cards

Buy a deck or two of cards to pack into the suitcase. Teach your child a few solitaire games to play by himself and some games to play with new friends. Besides the standards, such as Go Fish, Old Maid, Concentration, and War, teach him a few new games he may not know, such as Hearts, Crazy Eights, Doubt It, and 500 Rummy. If you've forgotten the rules, you can find them in card game books at the bookstore or library or even on the Internet. Toss in the card game book with the decks of cards, too.

Kite

Buy an inexpensive kite and hide it in the suitcase so that your child will discover it when she gets to camp. Let her put it

together, following the instructions, and then fly it with camp mates. Include lots of string so that it will really take off into the wild blue yonder and anything else the instructions require.

Frisbee Golf

Put a Frisbee in the suitcase so that your child can toss it around with his new friends. Teach him how to play Frisbee Golf before he goes off to camp, and then he can set up a game when he gets there. Designate some trees as goals and have the kids stand back a few yards, and then take turns trying to hit the goals with the Frisbees. Move on to the next tree after five tries if you don't hit the goal and keep score by counting how many times it takes to hit the goal. The player with the lowest score wins the game.

 Tip

Put your paper plate inside a Frisbee and it won't blow off the table.

Game and Puzzle Books

Head for the bookstore or magazine rack and pick up some puzzle books for your child to use during downtime. There are lots for kids, including crosswords, searchwords, jumblewords, logic puzzles, cryptograms, and other brain busters to keep your child thinking during the summer.

Hackey Sack

Buy a couple of Hackey Sacks, one for your child and one for a new friend. Then teach your child the basics of keeping the sack up in the air using only his feet. It takes practice, but she should be able to play fairly well after a few days. While she's at camp, she can teach others how to play, and then get a game going by kicking the Hackey Sack back and forth between friends.

Mad-Libs: Stories You Create Yourself

Mad-Libs are books of funny, fill-in-the-blank stories you create yourself. They're sold in most bookstores. Mad-Libs are always a hit with a group of kids and produce lots of laughs and good times. They also help kids keep up their reading skills. Mad-Libs are inexpensive, come in a variety of themes, and are easy to play during a break or when it's time to quiet down. You can also teach your child how to make up his own Mad-Libs game by replacing nouns, verbs, adjectives, and other words in magazine and newspaper stories.

Sports Equipment

Have your child take along some favorite pieces of his sporting equipment so that he can get a game going between activities. A softball, football, soccer ball, or basketball can be easily stuffed into the suitcase or backpack and will provide hours of fun for small or large groups of kids.

Water Balloons

Include a package or two of water balloons so that the kids can get wet and cool off on a hot day. Tell your child to get permission from the camp counselors before using them, and then fill them with water and attack!

Campfire Songs to Learn

Most camps have a campfire several times during the session, with chats, skits, stories, songs, snacks, and fun. Give your child a head start with the songs by practicing a few before she leaves for camp. She'll know all the words by heart when it comes time to sing and maybe even teach a few to the rest of the group. The two of you can even make up your own funny verses if you like. Here are some favorites with camp kids.

Annoying Song
(Sung to "Battle Hymn of the Republic")
I know a song that gets on everybody's nerves,
I know a song that gets on everybody's nerves,
I know a song that gets on everybody's nerves,
And this is how it goes . . .
(Repeat forever—or until you annoy everyone!)

Ants Go Marching
(Sung to "When Johnny Comes Marching Home Again")
The ants go marching one-by-one. Hurrah! Hurrah!
The ants go marching one-by-one. Hurrah! Hurrah!
The ants go marching one-by-one,
The little one stopped to suck his thumb,
And they all went marching
Down, around the town.

> The ants go marching two-by-two. Hurrah! Hurrah!
> The ants go marching two-by-two. Hurrah! Hurrah!

The ants go marching two-by-two,
The second one stopped to tie his shoe,
And they all went marching
Down, around the town.

The ants go marching three-by-three. Hurrah! Hurrah!
The ants go marching three-by-three. Hurrah! Hurrah!
The ants go marching three-by-three,
The third one stopped to climb a tree,
And they all went marching
Down, around the town.

The ants go marching four-by-four. Hurrah! Hurrah!
The ants go marching four-by-four. Hurrah! Hurrah!
The ants go marching four-by-four,
The fourth one stopped to close the door,
And they all went marching
Down, around the town.

The ants go marching five-by-five. Hurrah! Hurrah!
The ants go marching five-by-five. Hurrah! Hurrah!
The ants go marching five-by-five,
The fifth one stopped to do a jive,
And they all went marching
Down, around the town.

The ants go marching six-by-six. Hurrah! Hurrah!
The ants go marching six-by-six. Hurrah! Hurrah!
The ants go marching six-by-six,
The sixth one stopped to pick up sticks,
And they all went marching
Down, around the town.

The ants go marching seven-by-seven. Hurrah! Hurrah!
The ants go marching seven-by-seven. Hurrah! Hurrah!
The ants go marching seven-by-seven,
The seventh one stopped to go to Heaven,
And they all went marching
Down, around the town.

The ants go marching eight-by-eight. Hurrah! Hurrah!
The ants go marching eight-by-eight. Hurrah! Hurrah!
The ants go marching eight-by-eight,
The eighth one stopped to close the gate,
And they all went marching
Down, around the town.

The ants go marching nine-by-nine. Hurrah! Hurrah!
The ants go marching nine-by-nine. Hurrah! Hurrah!
The ants go marching nine-by-nine,
The ninth one stopped to check the time,
And they all went marching
Down, around the town.

The ants go marching ten-by-ten. Hurrah! Hurrah!
The ants go marching ten-by-ten. Hurrah! Hurrah!
The ants go marching ten-by-ten,
The tenth one stopped to start again,
And they all went marching
Down, around the town.

(Start again!)

Baby Bumble Bee

I'm bringing home my baby bumble bee. *(hold in closed hands)*
Won't my mommy be so proud of me!
I'm bringing home my baby bumble bee,
Oh, ee, it stung me! *(open hands)*

I'm squishing up my baby bumble bee. *(smash hands together)*
Won't my mommy be so proud of me!
I'm squishing up my baby bumble bee,
Oh, ee, it's stuck to me! *(shake hands)*

I'm licking up my baby bumble bee. *(pretend to lick hands)*
Won't my mommy be so proud of me!
I'm licking up my baby bumble bee,
Oh, ee, it's salty! *(stick out tongue)*

I'm throwing up my baby bumble bee. *(make throwing-up noise)*
Won't my mommy be so proud of me!
I'm throwing up my baby bumble bee,
Oh, ee, look at me! *(wipe off chest)*

Backwards Song

Well I walked up the door and I opened the stairs,
Said my pajamas and I put on my prayers,
Turned off the bed and jumped into the light,
All because he kissed me good night!

Well, I woke up next morning and I scrambled my shoes,
Shined up an egg and I toasted the news,
Buttered my tie and took another bite,
All because he kissed me good night!

Be Kind to Your Fine-Feathered Friends

Be kind to your fine-feathered friends,
For a duck may be somebody's mother.
They live in a swamp all alone,
Where the weather is always damp.
You may think that this is the end,
Well, it is! *(suddenly stop singing!)*

Here's an alternate ending you might prefer:

Be kind to your fine-feathered friends,
For a duck may be somebody's mother.
They live in a swamp all alone,
Where the weather is always damp.
You may think that this is the end,
It is, but to prove I'm a liar,
We're going to sing it again,
Only this time a little bit higher!
(Repeat the song in a higher voice)

Bingo!

Farmer Brown, he had a dog,
And Bingo was his name-o!
B-I-N-G-O,
B-I-N-G-O,
B-I-N-G-O,
And Bingo was his name-o!

(Sing the first line, then replace the last letter with a clap in the second verse, then the last two letters with two claps in the third verse, and so on, till you reach five claps.)

Boa Constrictor

I'm being eaten by a boa constrictor,
A boa constrictor, a boa constrictor.
I'm being eaten by a boa constrictor,
And I don't like it one little bit.
Oh, no, there goes my toe!
Oh, gee, he's got my knee!
Oh, my, there goes my thigh!
Oh, hum, there goes my bum!
Oh, darn, there goes my arm!
Oh, heck, he's got my neck!
Oh, gee, he's eaten me!

Cabin in the Woods

In a cabin in the woods, *(make a roof with hands)*
A little old man by the window stood, *(look through binoculars)*
Saw a rabbit hopping by, *(two-finger "ears" hop by)*
Scared as he could be. *(shake "ears")*
"Help Me, help me," the rabbit said, *(fling arms up and down)*
"Or the hunter will shoot me dead." *(shoot with fingers)*
"Come little rabbit, come with me," *(gesture "come" with hand)*
"Happy we will be!" *(pat the two-fingered bunny)*

Do Your Ears Hang Low?

Do your ears hang low? *(put backs of hands on ears, fingers down,
    to make ears)*
Do they wobble to and fro? *(sway fingers)*
Can you tie them in a knot? *(gesture tying hands in knot)*
Can you tie them in a bow? *(gesture tying bow)*

Can you throw them over your shoulder *(gesture throwing them over shoulder)*
Like a continental soldier? *(salute)*
Do your ears hang low? *(put backs of hands back on ears)*

Found a Peanut

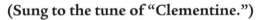

(Sung to the tune of "Clementine.")

Found a peanut, found a peanut, found a peanut, last night.
Last night, I found a peanut, found a peanut, last night.

Broke it open, broke it open, broke it open, last night.
Last night, I broke it open, broke it open, last night.

It was rotten, it was rotten, it was rotten, last night.
Last night, it was rotten, it was rotten, last night.

Ate it anyway, ate it anyway, ate it anyway, last night.
Last night, ate it anyway, ate it anyway, last night.

Got a stomachache, got a stomachache, got a stomachache, last night.
Last night, got a stomachache, got a stomachache, last night.

Called the doctor, called the doctor, called the doctor, last night.
Last night, called the doctor, called the doctor, last night.

Got a shot, got a shot, got a shot, last night.
Last night, got a shot, got a shot, last night.

Operation, operation, operation, last night.
Last night, operation, operation, last night.

Died anyway, died anyway, died anyway, last night.
Last night, died anyway, died anyway, last night.

Went to heaven, went to heaven, went to heaven, last night.
Last night, went to heaven, went to heaven, last night.

Wouldn't take me, wouldn't take me, wouldn't take me, last
  night.
Last night, wouldn't take me, wouldn't take me, last night.

Went the other way, went the other way, went the other way,
  last night.
Last night, went the other way, went the other way, last night.

Didn't want me, didn't want me, didn't want me, last night.
Last night, didn't want me, didn't want me, last night.

Was a dream, was a dream, was a dream, last night.
Last night, was a dream, was a dream, last night.

Woke up, woke up, woke up, last night.
Last night, woke up, woke up, last night.

Found a peanut, found a peanut, found a peanut, last night.
Last night I found a peanut, found a peanut, last night.
(Repeat, if you like.)

Gopher Guts

Great green gobs of grimy greasy gopher guts,
Mutilated monkey meat, dirty little birdie's feet.
Great green gobs of grimy greasy gopher guts,
And I forgot my spoon!

Hole in the Bottom of the Sea

(Sung to the tune, "If You're Happy and You Know It, Clap Your Hands.")

There's a hole in the bottom of the sea.
There's a hole in the bottom of the sea.
There's a hole, there's a hole,
There's a hole in the bottom of the sea.

There's a log in the hole in the bottom of the sea.
There's a log in the hole in the bottom of the sea.
There's a log, there's a log,
There's a log in the bottom of the sea.

There's a bump on the log in the hole in the bottom of the sea.
There's a bump on the log in the hole in the bottom of the sea.
There's a bump, there's a bump,
There's a bump in the bottom of the sea.

There's a frog on the bump on the log in the hole in the bottom of the sea.
There's a frog on the bump on the log in the hole in the bottom of the sea.
There's a frog, there's a frog.
There's a frog in the bottom of the sea.

There's a fly on the frog on the bump on the log in the hole in the bottom of the sea.
There's a fly on the frog on the bump on the log in the hole in the bottom of the sea.
There's a fly, there's a fly.
There's a fly in the bottom of the sea.

There's a wing on the fly on the frog on the bump on the log
in the hole in the bottom of the sea.
There's a wing on the fly on the frog on the bump on the log
in the hole in the bottom of the sea.
There's a wing, there's a wing.
There's a wing in the bottom of the sea.

There's a flea on the wing on the fly on the frog on the bump
on the log in the hole in the bottom of the sea.
There's a flea on the wing on the fly on the frog on the bump
on the log in the hole in the bottom of the sea.
There's a flea, there's a flea.
There's a flea in the bottom of the sea.

There's a hole in the bottom of the sea.
There's a hole in the bottom of the sea.
There's a hole, there's a hole,
There's a hole in the bottom of the sea.

Kookaburra

Kookaburra sits in the old gum tree,
Merry merry king of the bush is he.
Laugh, Kookaburra, laugh, Kookaburra,
Gay your life must be, ha ha ha!

> Kookaburra sits on an electric wire,
> Jumping up and down sets his butt on fire.
> Fry Kookaburra, fry Kookaburra,
> Tasty you will be, ha ha ha!

Kookaburra sits in the old split rail,
Pulling all the splinters out of his tail.
Ouch, Kookaburra, ouch, Kookaburra,
Sore your tail must be, ha ha ha!

> Kookaburra sits on the railroad tracks,
> Better get off or he'll be knocked flat.
> Run Kookaburra, run Kookaburra,
> Uh-oh—watch out! Splat!

Kumbaya

Kumbaya, my Lord, Kumbaya,
Kumbaya, my Lord, Kumbaya,
Kumbaya, my Lord, Kumbaya,
Oh, Lord, Kumbaya.

> Someone's singing, my Lord, Kumbaya,
> Someone's singing, my Lord, Kumbaya,
> Someone's singing, my Lord, Kumbaya,
> Oh, Lord, Kumbaya.

Someone's laughing, my Lord, Kumbaya,
Someone's laughing, my Lord, Kumbaya,
Someone's laughing, my Lord, Kumbaya,
Oh, Lord, Kumbaya.

> Someone's crying, my Lord, Kumbaya,
> Someone's crying, my Lord, Kumbaya,
> Someone's crying, my Lord, Kumbaya,
> Oh, Lord, Kumbaya.

Lady with the Alligator Purse

Miss Lucy had a turtle.
His name was Tiny Tim.
She put him in the bathtub
To teach him how to swim.

He drank up all the water.
He ate up all the soap.
He tried to eat the bathtub
But it wouldn't go down his throat.

Miss Lucy called the doctor.
Miss Lucy called the nurse.
Miss Lucy called the Lady
With the Alligator Purse.
"Mumps," said the doctor.
"Measles," said the nurse.
"Nothing," said the Lady
With the Alligator Purse.

Out walked the doctor.
Out walked the nurse.
Out walked the Lady
With the Alligator Purse.

"I mailed a comic book to my child every day, so he'd have a surprise in the mail and something to read at night in case he needed help getting to sleep. They were inexpensive and easy to mail, and my son loved them."
—*Maureen G.*

On Top of Spaghetti
(Sung to the tune of "On Top of Old Smokey.")

On top of spaghetti, all covered with cheese,
I lost my poor meatball when somebody sneezed.
It rolled off the table and onto the floor,
And then my poor meatball rolled out of the door.
It rolled through the garden and under a bush,
And then my poor meatball was nothing but mush.
The mush was as fertile, as fertile could be,
And later that summer, there sprouted a tree.
The tree was all covered with beautiful moss,
And on it grew meatballs in tomato sauce.

There's a Hole in My Bucket

There's a hole in my bucket, dear Liza, dear Liza.
There's a hole in my bucket, dear Liza, a hole.

> Then fix it, dear Henry, dear Henry, dear Henry.
> Then fix it, dear Henry, dear Henry, fix it.

With what shall I fix it, dear Liza, dear Liza?
With what shall I fix it, dear Liza, fix it?

> With a straw, dear Henry, dear Henry, dear Henry.
> With a straw, dear Henry, dear Henry, a straw.

But the straw is too long, dear Liza, dear Liza.
But the straw is too long, dear Liza, too long.

> Then cut it, dear Henry, dear Henry, dear Henry.
> Then cut it, dear Henry, dear Henry, cut it.

With what shall I cut it, dear Liza, dear Liza?
With what shall I cut it, dear Liza, with what?

> With a knife, dear Henry, dear Henry, dear Henry.
> With a knife, dear Henry, dear Henry, a knife.

But the knife is too dull, dear Liza, dear Liza.
But the knife is too dull, dear Liza, too dull.

> Then sharpen it, dear Henry, dear Henry, dear Henry.
> Then sharpen it, dear Henry, dear Henry, sharpen it.

With what shall I sharpen it, dear Liza, dear Liza?
With what shall I sharpen it, dear Liza, with what?

> With a stone, dear Henry, dear Henry, dear Henry.
> With a stone, dear Henry, dear Henry, a stone.

But the stone is too dry, dear Liza, dear Liza.
But the stone is too dry, dear Liza, too dry.

> Then wet it, dear Henry, dear Henry, dear Henry.
> Then wet it, dear Henry, dear Henry, wet it.

With what shall I wet it, dear Liza, dear Liza?
With what shall I wet it, dear Liza, with what?

> With water, dear Henry, dear Henry, dear Henry.
> With water, dear Henry, dear Henry, with water.

Well, how shall I carry it, dear Liza, dear Liza?
Well, how shall I carry it, dear Liza, carry it?

> In a bucket, dear Henry, dear Henry, dear Henry.
> In a bucket, dear Henry, dear Henry, a bucket.

But there's a HOLE IN MY BUCKET! dear Liza, dear Liza.
There's a HOLE IN MY BUCKET! dear Liza, a hole . . .

This Old Man

This old man, he plays one,
He plays knick-knack on my drum.
Knick-knack paddy whack,
Give a dog a bone,
This old man comes rolling home.

> This old man, he plays two,
> He plays knick-knack on my shoe.
> Knick-knack paddy whack,
> Give a dog a bone,
> This old man comes rolling home.

This old man, he plays three,
He plays knick-knack on my knee.
Knick-knack paddy whack,
Give a dog a bone,
This old man comes rolling home.

> This old man, he plays four,
> He plays knick-knack on my door.
> Knick-knack paddy whack,
> Give a dog a bone,
> This old man comes rolling home.

This old man, he plays five,
He plays knick-knack on my hive.
Knick-knack paddy whack,

Give a dog a bone,
This old man comes rolling home.

> This old man, he plays six,
> He plays knick-knack on my sticks.
> Knick-knack paddy whack,
> Give a dog a bone,
> This old man comes rolling home.

This old man, he plays seven,
He plays knick-knack up in heaven.
Knick-knack paddy whack,
Give a dog a bone,
This old man comes rolling home.

> This old man, he plays eight,
> He plays knick-knack on my gate.
> Knick-knack paddy whack,
> Give a dog a bone,
> This old man comes rolling home.

This old man, he plays nine,
He plays knick-knack on my vine.
Knick-knack paddy whack,
Give a dog a bone,
This old man comes rolling home.

> This old man, he plays ten,
> He play knick-knack over again.
> Knick-knack paddy whack,
> Give a dog a bone,
> This old man comes rolling home.

(Repeat, if you like)

Worms

Nobody likes me, everybody hates me.
I'm going down to the garden to eat worms.
Long thin slimy ones, short fat fuzzy ones,
Ooey gooey, ooey gooey worms.

Long thin slimy ones slip down easily.
Short fat fuzzy ones don't.
Short fat fuzzy ones stick to your teeth,
And the juice goes *(slurping noise)* down your throat.

Worms Crawl In

The worms crawl in,
The worms crawl out,
The worms crawl over
Your face and snout.

Your eyes bulge out,
Your teeth turn green,
Your pus runs out
Like a molten stream.

4

Heading Off and Coming Home

Getting Your Child to Camp Safely and Happily

This chapter addresses the bookends of the camp: getting your child there happily and making his or her coming home a time to celebrate. As a parent, this is your domain. Put some effort into both these events to begin the camping experience on a good note and end it by putting a big smile on your camper's face.

Choosing the Best Mode of Transportation

There are several issues to consider when you are deciding how to get your child to camp. First, of course, is distance. The camp may be so far away that driving is not an option.

If this is the case, you may be sending your child to camp by carpool, bus, or even on an airplane.

Safety Issues

Here are some tips for making sure your child arrives safely at his destination.

- Include any medication information that might be important to know while he's traveling, such as medic alert, allergic reactions, and so on.
- Have your child telephone you at intervals if the trip is long to make sure she's safe along the way. Give her a cell phone or calling card to make calling easier.
- Teach your child the rules about safety, such as Don't talk to strangers, Don't go with anyone you don't know, Don't leave the group, Don't travel by yourself, Don't go to the bathroom unattended, and so on.
- Don't overemphasize motion sickness, but provide him with medication or a patch, approved for his weight and age level, if necessary. Tell him not to read while traveling if he feels dizzy and to keep his eyes forward to help maintain equilibrium.

◆ Don't display your child's first name on his shirt or bag. This invites strangers to call your child by name, which may cause your child to think the person knows him and is safe. Instead, write your child's name, address, phone number, and destination information on a card and place it in your child's pocket, carry-on bag, or other safe spot.

If you are sending your child to camp in a car, here are some tips:

◆ Make sure all the seats in the vehicle have seatbelts.

◆ Check to see that the driver is experienced and over 18, with no driving violations.

◆ Look over the vehicle to see that it's generally in good condition, including the tires, mirrors, door locks, and so on.

◆ Ask the driver if there will be breaks, and let your child know when the breaks will come.

◆ Find out the driver's rules and go over them with your child so he understands what he can and can't do along the way.

If the bus will be her mode of transportation, check out these tips:

◆ Arrive early and talk with the bus driver about the fact that your child is traveling alone. Ask if your child can sit up front, near the driver, so he feels more secure.

◆ Provide a snack for the drive in case the bus doesn't make any stops along the way.

◆ Have your child telephone you when he arrives at his destination.

◆ Call ahead to make sure your child will be met at the bus depot on time.

- Provide some activities to keep your child occupied on the long trip.
- Tell your child not to leave the bus except under the supervision of the driver.

Finally, some children will need to go by airplane to their camp. Tips for traveling include the following:

- Call the airlines far ahead of time to find out how they handle children traveling alone, and let them know your situation.
- Arrive at the airport early so your child can board early or meet one of the flight attendants on the plane.
- Provide activities and snacks to keep your child occupied on the trip.
- Tell your child what to expect on the flight, such as air turbulence, snacks, a movie, and so on. Tell him where he's likely to find the lavatories, when he can take off his seatbelt, and what amenities the plane might provide.
- Make sure someone is at his destination to meet him on time.
- Tell him to call you when he arrives at his destination.
- Encourage him to speak to a flight attendant if he has any problems while on board. They're there to help.

"Make sure your child has his phone number and other emergency contacts, to make him feel secure. And be sure you have the phone number of the camp."
—Maria-Elena B.

Keeping Your Child Entertained on the Way

They say that getting there can be half the fun, but for kids, riding on a bus for a long time can be pretty uncomfortable. Whether your child is traveling to camp by car, bus, train, or plane, keeping him occupied and engaged will help him pass the time with little or no homesickness, travel sickness, or general anxieties about the upcoming camp experience. Here are some games and activities to help your child enjoy the trip almost as much as the camp.

Alphabet Adventure

Have your child watch for signs along the way, keeping an eye out for words that begin with each letter of the alphabet. Have him begin with "A" and work his way through "Z." As soon as he finds the entire alphabet, have him play again. He can do this alone or play with his seat mate.

Animal Hunt

Write a list of animals for your child to find on his ride to camp and assign a different number of points for each animal. For example, he gets 1 point for spotting a bird, 2 points for finding a dog, 3 for a cat, 4 for a cow, 5 for a horse, 6 for a sheep, 7 for a goat, 8 for a deer, 9 for a pig, and 10 for a skunk. Have him count up his points when he reaches his destination.

Backseat Bingo

Draw a bingo grid, five squares by five squares, and write the names of objects your child is likely to see along his trip, such as a bridge, a stop sign, an airplane, a grocery store, a cow, and so on. Have him try to get a Bingo by finding five in a row or have him try to fill the whole card by the time he reaches camp.

Counting Cars

Write down a list of popular cars on a sheet of paper (you can find brand names in the automobile want-ads section of your newspaper). Have your child try to find one of each make and model listed as he heads for camp.

Fifty States

Give your child paper and pencil and have him try to spot as many out-of-state plates as he can during his trip. Have him record each one as he keeps an eye out for all 50 states. To make it more interesting, assign more points to states farther away from your own. So if you live in California, you might assign 1 point to the states bordering California and 10 points for states on the East Coast, with varying points in between.

Hidden Words

At the top of a sheet of paper, write down a long word or short phrase related to going to camp, such as "Wilderness," "Camp Havalottafun," or "Don't forget to write!" Have your child write to find as many hidden words as he can within the word or phrase. For example, get him started with "Wilderness" and suggest "wild," "weird," "weed," "seed," "Nile," "side," and so on.

Literary License

Tell your child to see how many words he can make out of the license plates he sees on his journey, sounding out the letters to form a familiar word. For example, if a license plate reads "RDY," he might make the word "ready" or "ruddy." Or have him make up sentences using each letter on the plate, such as "Rattlesnakes Don't Yawn!"

Map It!

Send along a map of the trip so your child can follow the route to camp. Include some checkpoints for him to spot along the way to make it more fun and then mark off the distance so he can see how far he's come and how soon he'll be at his destination. Include a colored marker so he can mark the way, inch by inch and mile by mile. For added fun, have him collect points for each checkpoint he finds, such as a specific bridge, town, sign, or landmark.

Personalized Plates

Give your child paper and pencil and have him write down all the personalized license plates he sees as well as what he thinks they say. Have him bring the list home after camp and see whether the family can decipher all the plates, too.

Rainbow Row

Have your child try to find a car of each color of the rainbow—before he passes a police car. He must find a red, orange, yellow, purple, blue, and green car unless he sees a police car—then he loses all his colors and must start again.

See-a-Sign

Make a list of popular signs your child is likely to see on his route, such as "McDonalds," "Stop," "Gas," "Exit," "Wal-Mart," "School Zone," "Speed Limit 50," "Motel," and so on. Have him guess which sign he'll see the most, then have him check off each time he sees a listed sign. Have him count the totals to find out whether he guessed the sign that he'd see the most.

> "My son had his camp friends sign and decorate a pillow case. When he brought it home, we kept it right on his bed, and it reminded him each day of his fun time."
>
> —*Vanessa H.*

Welcome Home!

Before you know it, your little camper will be walking in the front door. A little dirty, perhaps, but glad to be home. Your smiling faces and open arms will probably be welcome enough, but in case you want to do something special to greet the long-lost camper, here are some suggestions to make that glad-to-be-home smile even bigger.

Big Banner

Make a big banner with the words "Welcome home, Camper (Child's Name)!" "Congratulations on Your First Summer at Camp!" or "We Missed You (Child's Name)!" Hang it on the garage door or front door so it's the first thing your child sees

when he arrives home. Make a couple more banners and place them around the inside of the house, such as in the kitchen, your child's room, and even the bathroom.

Bedroom Makeover

Redecorate your child's room and surprise him with a new bedspread, curtains, or furniture for a whole new makeover. Just make sure you don't remove anything he treasures, or you'll have to bring it back!

Surprise Party

Have a surprise party for your child, with friends and relatives waiting inside the house to greet him. Decorate the party room with a camp theme, write "Welcome Back Camper!" on the cake, and sing a few camp songs or play a few camp games for entertainment.

Message Center

Write a bunch of short messages on sticky notes and stick them all over your child's room to welcome him back. Your messages might include dozens of "Welcome Back!" greetings, updates on what's happened at home while the camper was gone, or questions your child has to answer about camp, such as "How was the food?" "Who was your best friend?" "Which counselor was the nicest?" and "What were your favorite activities?"

Decorate

Fill your child's room with balloons, streamers, banners, and other festive decorations. Float helium balloons from the ceiling, create a balloon canopy at the door, and tie balloons to the bed, drawers, and other furniture. Create a canopy over the bed using colorful crepe paper, swagged at the ceiling and draped down on the sides of the bed. Add colored lights and glow-in-the-dark stars on the ceiling and play band music.

Re-Create Camp

Set up a tent in the middle of your child's room to remind him of camp. Set out stuffed animals, play bird-sound CDs, and hang some snacks and laundry from a rope tied between two pieces of furniture. Let your child sleep overnight in the tent if he wants to.

Favorite Foods

Fix your child's favorite meal for that first day back, everything from his favorite drink to his favorite dessert. Or fix him some camp food, such as pork and beans and S'mores.

Information and Resources

Here are some informational resources you can send away for before your child goes to camp to help her enjoy the experience even more:

Bird Watching Booklet ($.50)
National Audubon Society
Information Services
950 Third Avenue
New York, NY 10022

First Aid Guide (free)
Johnson & Johnson
501 George Street
New Brunswick, NJ 08903

Insect Study Kit ($2.00)
National Audubon Society
Information Services
950 Third Avenue
New York, NY 10022

Ranger Rick Magazine ($14.00/year)
Ranger Rick
National Wildlife Federation
1412 16th Street NW
Washington, DC 20036

Wildlife Booklet ($.75)
Sierra Club
Public Affairs
730 Polk Street
San Francisco, CA 94109

Camp-Related Books

Here are some books that might help you with other camp-related issues:

Backyard Roughing It Easy: Unique Recipes for Outdoor Cooking by Dian Thomas

Campfire Songs by Irene Maddox

Cooking on a Stick: Campfire Recipes for Kids by Linda White

Kids Camp! by Laurie Carlson

Kids' Nature Book by Susan Milord

Kid's Summer Handbook by Jane Drake

Little Book of Campfire Songs by Brian Denington

Sleeping in a Sack: Camping Activities for Kids by Linda White

So You're Off to Summer Camp by Margaret Queen

Summer Camp Handbook by Christopher Thurber

Totally Camping Cookbook by Helene Siegel

Ultimate Summer Camp Guide by Devra Speregen

Part II

Kid's Guide

Welcome to camp! You and your parents have done a great job of finding the right camp and preparing for the exciting experience. You've packed everything you need—and more. No doubt you'll also receive a few surprises in the mail.

But now that you're finally there, the adventure is really about to begin. You're probably excited, nervous, eager to get started, and a little worried about what's to come. No need to worry. Camp will be over before you know it, and by the time it ends, you'll probably regret having to leave. If you have a touch of homesickness, you'll barely remember what that felt like in a few days. And you're going to have experiences and memories that will last a lifetime, not to mention all the great new friends you'll be meeting. So let's get started. It's time for camp!

5

Your First Day

Dealing with Homesickness

Many kids experience a little homesickness when they first arrive at camp. It's a strange new environment, very different from home, so you may feel a little uncomfortable in the beginning. And the people you meet are strangers to you—at first. It's these differences that cause some kids to miss home and family. But soon you'll become familiar with your new temporary home away from home, meet new friends, and have a great time doing all the activities the camp has planned.

But first, let's talk about homesickness. It does exist for many kids, even temporarily, and talking about it actually helps you deal with it. If you're not homesick at all, you can skip this chapter or come back to it if you're feeling lonely at some point during camp. But if you're already beginning to miss your own bedrooms, parents, friends, pets, and even sisters and brothers, here's how to deal with homesickness.

Get Those Feelings Out

The best thing to do is to figure out if you're really feeling homesick. You may feel kind of upset, a little sad, perhaps scared, or even panicky—these are all signs of homesickness. You might even experience a stomachache, a headache, shaky hands, and a little dizziness. All of this is *normal*. Your feelings control your body and can cause you to feel physically sick as well as emotionally frightened. Once you've determined the cause of your feelings, you're halfway to dealing with them. Keep in mind that you're not really sick like having the flu, so you don't need medicine. And you're not going to die of homesickness—no one ever has.

Just like a regular illness, those uncomfortable feelings should disappear over time—with the right treatment. It begins by getting those feelings out. Talk to yourself (better not talk out loud, or everyone will think you're crazy, too!). Talk to your tent mates about their feelings. Talk to your camp counselors. You'll find they have felt the same way you are feeling now—and they overcame it as well. You might even write down your feelings in your journal, and then check back in a day or two and see how your feelings change each day.

Make New Friends

One of the best ways to overcome homesickness is to make new friends. Sooner or later, you're going to make friends at camp, so it might as well be sooner. That way, you'll not only help overcome your homesickness, but you'll also have a bunch of new friends! Here are some ways to help you make friends when you arrive at camp.

Say Something

Start a conversation with the kid nearby. Talk about something that's about to happen at camp, such as "I hear we're going swimming today in the lake." Or ask a question, such as "Do you know if we get to go horseback riding here?" That will get the conversation going, especially if you ask a question. You might also talk about the camp in general, such as "I've heard this camp has pretty good food" or "What cabin are you assigned to?" You can also talk about your feelings, such as "I'm so excited to be here, but I'm also a little nervous"

"About halfway into the week, I sent a tin of home-made chocolate chip cookies to my daughter using overnight mail. I made sure to include enough for all the kids in her group, and I added a note asking my daughter to share. She got compliments the rest of the week on those cookies. Everyone knew her as the 'cookie girl,' so she made a lot of friends." —*Vicki S.*

or "I'm not so good at diving. I hope we don't have to go off the high dive!" Or begin a conversation by saying something about what you enjoy. That way, you'll discover whether you have anything in common with your new friend, such as "I love hiking. Have you done any rock climbing?" or "I hope they serve pizza here. Do you like pepperoni?"

Give a Compliment

Kids will respond to you when they hear you say something nice, such as a compliment or a word of encouragement. Notice something about your potential new friend and say something nice, such as "I really like your T-shirt! Where did you get it?" or "That's a cool bracelet. Did you make it?" You can comment on the other campers' clothes, hair, sunglasses, shoes, backpack, jewelry, or other characteristics, such as eyes, strength, pleasant smile, or cute laugh.

Kid Around

Make a joke and get a laugh—that's a great way to make a new friend. You can kid about yourself by saying something like "I

wonder where they're keeping Shrek in this place?" or "The most hiking I've done is to the mailbox!" Or you can make a joke about your surroundings, such as "This camp looks like Disneyland's Adventureland! Are these rocks real?" or "I heard the food tastes like cardboard. I like pepperoni on my cardboard." Just be careful not to make fun of others—that's not funny, it's mean, and it's the worst way to try to make friends. They may think you're laughing at them behind their backs. So keep the jokes friendly, not cruel.

Be Interested

At camp, you have the opportunity not only to meet new kids but also to learn something new about other people. Although people are similar in most ways, there are differences, and these differences make us interesting. When you begin talking with another camper, show interest in what he's saying or doing and be a good listener. Ask questions, make comments, make eye contact, nod your head, then share similar experiences that show you can relate. For example, if a camper is whittling some wood, you might give him a compliment on his project, then ask him how he learned whittling, what he's making, and whether he'll teach you how to whittle. Then offer to teach him something that you know, such as how to climb a tree, make a sun hat, or play a card game.

Find a Loner

If you're having trouble making friends or you're a little on the shy side, there's probably another kid at camp who hasn't made friends yet, either, so look around and see whether you spot anyone standing alone or playing by himself. Then go on over and say "Hi," introduce yourself, ask a question, and get that new friendship started. You'll be a lot happier if you find even one new friend. And so will the other kid.

Be a Good Friend

The best way to make friends is to be a good friend yourself. Kids can sense whether you're a nice person, treat others fairly, know how to cooperate and get along with others, are a good sport, and respect others' privacy and property. If you can't be a good friend to others, you'll have trouble keeping the friends that you make. Be honest, be respectful, and be nice. That's all it takes.

Stay Busy– Get Involved

Another way to cope with homesickness is to keep busy. Most of the time, the camp activities will take care of that. It's the counselors' job to provide lots of things to do throughout the day and evening so that you enjoy every minute of the experience. But sometimes you might have free time or may not want to participate in a particular activity, and that may cause boredom. When you're bored, you begin to think about all the things you miss about home, and that leads to homesickness. If you keep busy, you won't have time to think about anything but the fun you're having. Here are some ways to keep yourself occupied during camp.

Try a New Activity

If there's an activity you aren't interested in, the camp will probably provide some alternate activities that may be more to your liking. Try something new, such as a physical sport or arts and crafts activity, to see whether you enjoy it before deciding you're just not interested. Sometimes you'll discover you like something you didn't think you would simply because you've never had the chance to experience it. If bird watching sounds boring, whittling sounds too difficult, or rock climbing sounds scary, give it a try anyway and find out for yourself before you make up your mind.

Get a Game Going

When you have a break from the camp activities, get out one of the games you brought from home (or see whether the camp has a collection of games), then start a game with another camper. You'll be surprised how quickly a game gathers kids together. Or get out a ball and start throwing it around. Soon you'll have others joining you to share in the fun. If it's lights out or time to take a hike, leave the game set up as it is and rejoin it when you get another break. Try some new games

"My friend and I liked to take on new names when we went to camp. We'd tell the counselors that Colleen and Janice were our given names but that our nicknames were Laverne and Shirley or whatever personalities we picked for that summer. It was fun to be a totally new person for a week or two."   —*Colleen C.*

that other kids have with them and teach them the ones that you've brought along.

Write in Your Journal

Quiet time is the perfect time to catch up with your journal. Jot down what you did that day so that you'll remember to tell your family when you get home. Share your feelings about the camp and the people (but don't write anything too negative in case they happen to read it!). Talk about what you miss and what you look forward to when you return home. Write about the things you most enjoy at camp and what you'll miss about it when you get home. And list the things you'll want to do when you get back home, such as write your camp friends, give your room a makeover, learn to tie knots, and so on.

Start a Collection or Scrapbook

While you're at camp, start a new collection or add to a collection you already have. You might want to collect unusual rocks, a variety of leaves and flowers, pictures of nature, signatures, camp flyers, pinecones, oddly shaped nature items, and so on. Or work on your scrapbook and fill in a page or two each day with mementos of camp.

Help the Counselors

Ask your favorite counselor whether there's something you can do to help out around the camp. Doing something productive makes you feel useful and needed and keeps you from thinking about home. It's also a great way to learn new skills and meet some kids. You might even think about becoming a camp counselor yourself one day since you'll soon know what it's like to be a camper.

Write Letters

Another way to deal with homesickness is to write your family and friends each day and tell them what's going on at camp. If you write down your experiences and adventures, you'll remind yourself of all the fun you're having and that you're lucky to have the opportunity to get away from home. Besides that, your family will be pleased to see that you're doing well. Let them know you miss them, but try not to overdo the homesickness routine—you don't want to make your family feel too bad! Keep your sense of humor when you write and see whether you can come up with creative and funny ways to talk about the camp food, counselors, and campfire.

Plan Your Goals

Look over the next day's activities and pick out what looks like the most fun, then think about how much you're going to enjoy it. Picture yourself playing, hiking, swimming, or whatever and think about what you want to get out of the experience. After you set your goals, remind yourself of them at the end of the day to see how many goals you met. You'll feel good about yourself and your camp experience when you realize how much you've accomplished and learned.

Keep It Real

Finally, keep camp in perspective. It's not going to last forever. In fact, you'll be surprised how quickly the time passes. You will live through the experience—that's a promise. Remember, no one has ever died of going to camp. And you will return home. Your parents haven't secretly moved away, leaving no forwarding address. They're as eager to see you as you are to see them. So get the most of your camp experience. After all, when it's over, you'll have to go home. By then, you may not want to!

6

Tent Fun

Activities, Games, and Gags

When it's time to hit the sack, you'll probably be tuckered out from a full day of fun and fall asleep as soon as your head hits the pillow. But if you're not tired, here are some things to do in your cabin or tent until you drift off to dreamland.

Tent-Time Activities

When you get a chance to spend some time in your tent with your camp mates, here are some fun things to do.

Fortune-Telling

All you need is a plain sheet of paper to make one of these Fortune Tellers (you might know it as a Cootie Catcher), then you can predict your tent mate's future:

1. Get a square sheet of paper. (If the paper isn't square, fold the paper into a triangle and trim the excess, then unfold it, and you'll have a square.)
2. Fold the paper in half the opposite way to make another triangle, then unfold that.
3. Fold the corners to the center so they meet.
4. Turn the paper over and fold those corners into the center.
5. Fold the paper in half to make a rectangle.
6. Unfold, then refold again the opposite way.
7. Unfold and write camp-related words on the four top squares, such as "woodchuck," "beaver," "squirrel," and "skunk."
8. Under the folds, write eight camp activities in the sections, such as "hiking," "swimming," "whittling," "cooking," "boating," "crafting," "chopping," and "riding."
9. Under those folds, write funny fortunes for the campers, such as "You will get poison oak!" "You will meet a cute camper!" "You will find dinosaur bones!" "You will stay at camp forever!" and so on.
10. Stick your fingers into the folded corners to create your Fortune Teller Cootie Catcher.

11. Have a friend choose one of the camp animals, such as "woodchuck."
12. Count out the letters in the word as you open and close the Fortune Teller.
13. Have a friend pick a word on the inside just under his selection, such as "hiking."
14. Count out the letters for that word, then open up the fold and read the fortune hidden underneath.

Hand Reading

Take a look at a tent mate's hand and tell her you're going to read her fortune by studying the lines and marks on her palm and hand. (This is only for fun—don't take it seriously!) Here's how to read her fortune:

1. The line that runs across the top of the palm is the "Love Line." If it's smooth, you'll have a long romance. If it's broken, the romance will be rocky.
2. The line in the middle is the "Fortune Line." If it's long and smooth, you will be rich. If it's short or broken, you will be poor.
3. The line going down the palm is the "Life Line." If the line is long and smooth, you'll have a long life. If the line is short or broken, you'll have a short life.
4. If you have short nails, you'll work hard in life. If you have long nails, you'll have an easy life.
5. If you have any scars on your hand, you'll have lots of adventures. If your hand is smooth, you'll have a quiet life.

6. If you can see the veins on the back of the hand and they stick out a little, you'll be a sensitive and caring person. If you can't see the veins well and the back of the hand is smooth, you'll be a cold and crabby person.

7. When you stretch your fingers of one hand out flat and press them together, check to see whether you can see space between the fingers. Each space represents a big surprise in life.

8. If your fingers are double-jointed, you'll be flexible and easygoing. If you're not double-jointed, you'll be strict and hard.

9. Make up fortunes for the other lines and marks on your hands to predict things like how many children you'll have, what type of job you'll get, and what your marriage will be like.

Mind Reading

Impress your camp mates with your amazing mind-reading skills, but you'll need a little help with this one! Choose a camp mate to play the trick with you and let him know what to do. Here's how you play:

1. Close your eyes and have someone in the tent point to something, such as a sleeping bag, some soap, a backpack, or a shoe.

"Write up Truth or Dare cards before you go to camp. It's a great way to make friends and to get to know your friends better. Just don't make the dares too wild." —*Teresa L.*

2. Open your eyes and have your partner ask you a question about something in the tent. Here's the trick: He must begin the sentence with the first letter of the selected object. And he must not point to the selected object until it's been spelled out. For example, if someone pointed to a shoe, he might ask you, "So, do you think it's this jacket?" as he points to a jacket (not the shoe).

   His second choice might be, "Have you decided it's this bag?" Next he might ask, "Oh, I'll bet you think it's this sock." And finally he might say, "Even this box could be it, right?" Keep saying, "No!" to each question. In the meantime, put the letters together: S-H-O-E.

3. When your partner finally points to the selected object, after having spelled it out using the sentences, you say, "Yes, it's the shoe!"

Belly Button Art

Get out your colored markers to create this work of body art. Then draw a masterpiece where no one except the wearer and the artist will see the finished product when it's covered up:

1. Using colored markers, take turns drawing designs around each other's belly buttons. You might make a flower, a sun, a heart, a snowflake, a hexagon, a star, a sun ray, or even a funny animal face, using the navel as the mouth or nose.

2. Use a variety of colors to make the decoration vivid and bright.

3. Take pictures of the designs so you'll have a record of them when the colors wash off or fade.

Body Tattoos

Create your own temporary tattoos that may even last the week—if you patch them up a bit when they start to fade:

1. Think about what kind of design you want. You might like a camp-related design, such as a beaver or squirrel, a picture of your tent or cabin, your camp name, the camp symbol, or a leaf or flower design.
2. Draw a sample of the design on a piece of paper.
3. Think about where you want the tattoo, such as on your ankle, your arm, your back, or your foot.
4. Have your camp mate copy the design onto your body using an ink pen or do it yourself if you can reach the spot.
5. If you have colored ink pens, make your tattoo colorful. If you have only a black or blue pen, keep the design simple and fill in the spaces with colored markers if you have them.
6. Enjoy your temporary tattoo—until it's time for swimming or showers. If it fades, you can redo it each night.

Funny Feet

Turn your socks into entertaining Funny Feet and put on a bedtime show with your camp mates:

1. Find some clean socks—if you can!
2. Put one sock on your (nondominant) hand and draw a funny face with colored markers.

3. Take the sock off and put on the other sock. Turn it into another goofy guy using the pens.

4. Put the socks on your feet so the funny face is on the top.

5. Lie down on your sleeping bags parallel to each other, heads on pillows, so you can all see your funny feet.

6. Put on a silly show by wiggling your feet and talking in funny voices.

7. Play some music and have the feet dance to the beat.

8. For added fun, have your camp mates draw the funny faces—while the socks are on your feet! But watch out: This tickles, and you may end up with really funny faces—and a stomachache from laughing!

Nail Salon

After you're all ready for bed, take some time for a manicure and give your nails a makeover:

1. Get out the bottles of nail polish you brought from home.

2. Do each other's nails using a variety of colors and styles. Try multicolors, half-and-half colors, designs, letters, and dots.

3. Add some glitter for added sparkle.

4. Show off your nails—and keep them clean! But don't let them stop you from having fun in the dirt.

Chinny-Chin-Chum

This will give you the giggles, so be prepared to laugh:

1. Lie down on your back on your sleeping bag.
2. Have a camp mate sit at your head.
3. Have her draw some eyes near the bottom of your chin.
4. Have her draw a nose between the eyes and your real lips, using colored markers.
5. Highlight your lips with lipstick or a red marker.
6. Tie a bandanna over your face so that only your lips and chin show.
7. When your upside-down Chin Chum is ready, have your camp mates sit on the floor at your head and have a chat with them. Watch them start to giggle as you keep your Chin Chum talking!
8. Take turns making Chin Chums and entertaining each other.

Camp Characters

Become a part of nature while you're at camp and find your new identity. Here are some ways to adapt your name:

1. Write your name on a piece of paper. Scramble the letters to create a new camp name. For example, if your name is Matt Warner, rearrange the letters to form "Wanter Tram" or "Mane Tarter."
2. Choose a name from one of the animals around camp, such as "Squirrel," "Beaver," "Bear," or "Skunk."
3. Create an Indian name by combining several nature terms, such as "Tall-as-a-Tree," "Swims-in-the-Creek,"

"Flying Bear," "Skunk's Tail," "Sings-Like-a-Bird," "Whispering Flower," "Happy Squirrel," "Jumping Frog," or "Walks-Like-a-Deer."

4. Make your name out of nature symbols. For example, for the name "Becca," draw a vertical stick with two acorns on the right side for the "B," part of a fence with one vertical post and three horizontal posts on the right for the "E," a brook in the shape of a "C," then another "C," and a tepee for the "A."

Card Games

You probably know some basic card games, so here are some ways to make those old favorites more interesting while you're at camp.

Wacky War

Instead of playing regular War, try this twist:

1. Give each suit a category, such as Hearts = "Girl's Names," Diamonds = "Colors," Clubs = "Flowers," and Spades = "Trees."

"Always sleep with your clothes for the next day inside your sleeping bag (but not as a pillow). Then they are warm to put on and you don't have to spring out of your sleeping bag on a frosty morning in your PJs to go get them."   —Ann P.

2. Pass out all the cards to the players, face down.

3. Players flip over their top cards at the same time. But instead of winning by having the highest card, the players who match suits must call out something from the corresponding category. For example, if two or more players turn over hearts, they must race to call out a girl's name, such as "Mary!"

4. The player who calls it out first wins the round and the pile of cards.

5. No one may call out the winning words again, so if "Mary" has been used to win, players cannot use it again. They must come up with a new girl's name.

6. Here's an added twist: If two or more players turn over the same *numbers,* that takes priority over suits, and those players must race to call out a word from, say, the category of "animals."

7. When you get good at the game, change all the categories. Try not to get mixed up!

Funny Fish

Here's a fun version of plain old Fish:

1. Deal out seven cards to each player.

2. Take turns asking each other for cards as you try to complete pairs.

3. Here's a twist: Ask for the cards in Spanish, sign language, mime, or pig Latin.

Crawlspace Concentration

Jazz up Concentration with a little creativity:

1. Turn all the cards face down on a flat surface.
2. Take turns flipping over two cards at a time to see whether you can find a match.
3. Here's a twist: Each time a space is created, move the cards inward to fill that space. This will make it even harder to remember where those overturned cards were!

Crazy Mixed-Up Eights

Here's a crazy mixed-up version of Crazy Eights:

1. Pass out eight cards to each player.
2. Turn the rest of the pile face down, with one card face up next to it.
3. Players take turns placing a card from their hands onto the face-up pile by trying to match either the suit or the number.
4. If a player can't play a card, he must draw from the face-down pile until he finds a card that matches.
5. The first player to get rid of all the cards is the winner.
6. Here's a twist: Instead of making 8s crazy each time, change the crazy number for each new game.
7. If you get mixed up and accidentally play the wrong number, you lose a turn and must draw a card!

Card Tricks

Amaze your mates with some sleight of hand.

That's Your Card!

Baffle your camp mates with this card trick:
1. Have your camp mate shuffle a deck of cards.
2. When you get the cards back, secretly and carefully glance at the bottom card. This is called "the marked card."
3. Separate the deck into five piles, each one face down, and remember which pile has the marked card.
4. Ask your camp mate to lift the top card off any pile, look at it, and put it back down on the pile.
5. Pick up the pile with the marked card and put it on top of the pile your camp mate selected.
6. Pile up the remaining cards and have your camp mate cut the deck.
7. Slowly look through cards. When you find the marked card, the very next card will be the one selected by your camp mate. Show him the card and watch his amazed reaction.

Pick a Card, Any Card!

Here's another amazing trick to astound your friends:

1. Count out 21 cards and set the rest of the cards aside.
2. Deal out the cards face up in three piles of seven cards each and spread out in a row so that all the cards are visible.

3. Ask your camp mate to mentally choose a card and to tell you which row it's in but not which card it is.
4. Carefully slide the cards back into their three stacks.
5. Collect the three piles, placing the pile with selected card in between the other two piles.
6. Deal the cards face up in three piles of seven each again, being sure to move from left to right, putting one card on each pile each time you deal and making sure each card shows.
7. Ask your camp mate to point to the pile that contains his selected card but not to tell you which card it is.
8. Gather the cards carefully again, placing the pile with the selected card between other two piles.
9. Deal the cards into a single pile, face down, counting them silently until you reach card number 11. Turn it over. That will be your camp mate's selected card.

Paper and Pencil Games

All you need for these games—besides your brain—are paper and pencil and a pal or two.

Triple Tic-Tac-Toe

You probably know how to play Tic-Tac-Toe. In fact, it's not a very exciting game in its traditional form. Here's how to make it exciting:

1. Draw three Tic-Tac-Toe grids right next to each other.
2. Play all three games at once!

Hangman's Fortune

Double the puzzle fun with a game of Hangman's Fortune, a combination of Hangman and Wheel of Fortune:

1. Think of a common phrase, such as "Love makes the world go around."
2. Write it down without anyone seeing it.
3. Cross out the vowels so that it reads "L V M K S TH W RLD G R ND."
4. On another sheet of paper, draw a hangman's noose.
5. Underneath the noose, draw a line for each consonant, running the letters all together. The phrase above would look like this: _ _ _ _ _ _ _ _ _ _ _ _ _ _ _.
6. Have your camp mate guess consonants, one at a time, and try to fill in the lines.
7. When he has enough letters filled in and thinks he can solve the puzzle, let him try to guess the phrase. It won't be easy with all the letters run together and the vowels missing!
8. If he's hung by the Hangman before he can solve the puzzle, he loses the game.

Blind Dots and Boxes

If you don't know how to play Dots and Boxes, it's simple. Then we make it harder:

1. Make a grid of dots, 10 across by 10 down.
2. To play the game, take turns drawing a line between two dots.

3. Keep connecting the dots as you try to complete a box—but watch out that your opponent doesn't complete one!

4. Each time you complete a box by drawing one line, you get another turn.

5. To make the game more challenging, close your eyes when it's your turn to connect two dots.

6. If you miss either of the dots, you lose a turn.

Four-Letter Words

How many four-letter words can you guess?

1. Write a four-letter word at the top of a sheet of paper, such as "tent," and have your camp mate do the same.

2. Fold over the top of the paper to cover the word so your partner can't see it and vice versa.

3. Write down another four-letter word underneath your hidden word, such as "camp," and announce the word to your partner.

4. He must tell you how many letters in your word are in his hidden word. For example, if his hidden word is "swim" and you guess "camp," he would say "one" because there's an "m" in both "swim" and "camp."

5. Caution: Your partner should *not* tell you which letter it is. That's for you to figure out.

6. Take turns saying four-letter words to find out how many letters are the same. Write down the number of letters each time and come up with new words to ask your partner. By elimination, you should be able to figure out all four letters.

7. When you have all four letters, all you have to do is unscramble them to figure out your partner's hidden word.

8. When you've conquered four-letter words, try five-letter words!

Flashlight Fun

When it gets dark, turn on the flashlights for some nighttime fun.

Have a Séance

See if you can bring back some long-lost souls. Just don't creep yourself out too much, or you'll never get to sleep!

1. Everyone sits Indian style in a circle in the dark.

2. Turn on the flashlights so they shine up on your faces.

3. Hold hands and think of some famous dear departed person you want to chat with, such as Joan of Arc, George Washington, or Albert Einstein.

4. Have your camp mates ask a question to the dear departed.

5. Use a funny voice and answer the question, pretending to be the long-lost soul.

"Don't forget to send extra batteries with the flashlight. Your child is likely to use the flashlight a lot during camp, and those batteries won't last forever. Tape the replacements together, tuck them in the suitcase, and then tell your child where you've put them so he can find them easily."   —*Barbara S.*

Shadow Shapes

Make some spooky shapes in the tent shadows:

1. When the tent is completely dark, turn on a flashlight and shine it on the side of the tent.
2. Have a camp mate hold up a hand and make shadow shapes.
3. See whether the others can guess what the shapes are supposed to be.

Shooting Star

Have you ever seen a shooting star inside your tent? It only happens once in a blue moon:

1. Get into your sleeping bags and turn on your flashlights.
2. Choose one player to be "It."
3. The rest of the players shine their lights around the tent, while the player who is "It" must try to tag them with his own flashlight beam.
4. Take turns being "It."
5. You can also play Follow the Leader by having "It" move his flashlight beam around the tent while the rest of the players try to follow the beam as it moves.

Other Games to Play with Your Tent Mates

These tried-and-true games are always fun.

Jacks. Bring a couple of sets of Jacks to play with your friends at camp and get a Jacks tournament started.

Marbles. Take along a bag of marbles and make up same games, such as marble pool, marble bowling, marble toss, and marble tag.

Charades. All you need is paper and pencil for Charades. Divide into teams and write down some movie, song, and book titles. Go over the rules and the gestures ahead of time, then put the titles in a hat and take turns showing off your miming skills for your team to guess.

Dominoes. Set up a game of Dominoes with the tiles you've tucked into your suitcase or make up your own dominoes by cutting out rectangles and making dots.

Code One. Gather your camp mates for a Code One planning session so you can "talk" to one another without others knowing what you're saying. Here are some codes to get you started:

Wiggle two fingers = "Let's get going."
Pat your chin = "I'm hungry—got any food?"
Shake your hands = "I'm scared!"
Pat your heart = "That guy/girl is so hot!"

Pat your cheek = "I'm tired."

Thumbs up = "Let's do it."

Make up your own gestures for some of the things you want to say while you're at camp. Or make up crazy words or sounds to use instead of real ones to communicate secretly with your camp mates, such as the following:

"Rabbit hop" = "Let's get going."

"Chicken Feed" = "I'm hungry—got any food?"

"Baa-gawk!" = "I'm scared!"

"Ssssssss" = "That guy/girl is so hot!"

"Hibernation time" = "I'm tired."

"Fly like an eagle" = "Let's do it."

Gags for Giggles and Laughs

No camp is complete without a few harmless gags. Just be careful not to hurt anyone, or the gags won't be funny, and you may lose a new friend. And if someone plays a gag on you, be a good sport!

Freckle Face

While you're at camp, why not try on a few freckles for fun? Use an eyebrow pencil or brown marker and give yourself and your friends some cheeks full of dots. Then surprise your counselor—and yourself when you look in the mirror.

It's Contagious!

Here's a fun gag that will spread like a rash through the camp if you're not careful. While your camp mate is asleep, dot his face with red marker or lip pencil. When he wakes up, gasp and show him a mirror. He'll think he's broken out in measles! Or dot your own face and give your counselor a scare!

Chameleon Clothes

Play a game with your camp mates and see how well they notice details. Pick two players and have the rest of the players close their eyes. While everyone's eyes are closed, the two players exchange one article of clothing, such as a shirt, a hat, a bracelet, a hair clip, a vest, socks, shoes, and so on. Tell the others to open their eyes and try to guess what was switched. Have some fun with the rest of your campers the next day. Trade an article of clothing with a camp mate and see how long it takes someone to notice.

7

Over the Coals

Snazzy Campfire Snacks

Most of your campfire meals will be planned by the camp cooks, but you can add your own touches or suggest some new treats to try and add a little pizzazz to your pizzas and sizzle to your S'mores.

Traditional S'mores

It's not a campfire without a marshmallow roast and those sweet, gooey S'mores. But you can add sizzle to those traditional S'mores with a few fun additions. Then think up some more ways of jazzing up the classic snack. (You know why they call them "S'mores," of course—because you always want "some more!")

1. Toast a marshmallow over the coals until lightly browned. (Be careful not to burn it!)

2. Break a graham cracker rectangle in half to form two squares.
3. Place half a chocolate bar on one half of the graham cracker.
4. Add the toasted marshmallow and press the other graham cracker on top to make an ooey gooey chocolate-marshmallow sandwich.

Variations: Add peanut butter or a sliced banana. Or dip the finished S'more in chocolate sauce. Try substituting a mint chocolate bar for the regular chocolate bar. Or use large cookies in place of the graham crackers.

Banana Boats

Turn plain old bananas into a warm delicious dessert, and then add any extras that sound good:

1. Peel one side of a banana, leaving the rest intact.
2. Slice the banana while it's still in the peel and remove every other chunk. (Feel free to eat the chunks you remove.)
3. Fill the empty spaces with chocolate chips and mini-marshmallows.
4. Replace the peel, wrap the banana in foil, and place on the coals for about 10 minutes, until the chocolate and marshmallow have melted. Your Banana Boat will be hot, so eat it carefully!
5. You might also want to add chopped nuts, coconut, raisins, peanut butter chips, broken candy bar bits, or cherries.

Apple Scramble

Fill an apple and put it on the fire for a toasty Apple Scramble:

1. Core an apple, removing all the seeds.
2. Mix a tablespoon of peanut butter with a few raisins and chopped nuts.
3. Fill the apple hollow with the mixture.
4. Wrap in foil and heat on the campfire for about 10 minutes, until warm.
5. Allow to cool, then eat it up.
6. Think about other treats you can put inside the apple.

Orange Muffins

Start the day with sunshine—in the form of an Orange Muffin:

1. Cut an orange in half and remove the pulp.
2. Fill the orange shell with muffin mix.
3. Set the orange halves on the grill and bake about 20 to 25 minutes, until a toothpick comes out clean.
4. Allow to cool, then enjoy.

"Don't eat too many S'mores. I ate more than I should have and was sick all night long. To this day I can't stand the smell, taste or thought of S'mores."

—*Susan W.*

Eight-Legged Octopus

Turn a hot dog into a creature from beneath the sea. Funny how it still tastes like a hot dog:

1. Insert a stick into one end of hot dog, pushing it up about one-third of the way.
2. Cut the other end lengthwise into fourths to make four "legs."
3. Roast the legs until they sizzle and curl.
4. Remove the stick and insert it into the end with the legs.
5. Cut the other end into four legs and roast until they sizzle and curl.
6. Remove the Octopus from the heat and gobble it up.

Walking Salad

Take your lunch with you on your next hike.

1. Cut the top off an apple and save the top.
2. Then core the apple (which means cutting out the inside core and seeds). Throw the core away.
3. Next, dig out most of the white part of the apple and cut into small pieces. Leave as much of the of the apple shell (skin) intact as you can.
4. Mix the chopped-up apple with some of your trail mix or with some raisins, grated cheese, nuts or seeds and a little mayonnaise, if you have it.
5. Stuff the mixture into the apple shell and put the top back on.
6. Wrap the apple in foil and eat it on your hike.

Bugs on a Log

Turn plain old celery sticks into tasty treats that you can munch on the trail or in the tent.

1. Cut the ends off of a clean celery stick.
2. Fill the celery stick with spreadable cheese, cream cheese, or peanut butter.
3. Add some raisins, nuts, seeds, or trail mix on top.
4. Crunch and munch.

Burrito Brunch

Make your breakfast "to-go" with a filled tortilla wrap.

1. Heat a flour tortilla on the grill or just leave it cold.
2. Fill the tortilla with scrambled eggs, sausage, bacon, shredded cheese, or anything else that is served for breakfast.
3. Roll up the tortilla and enjoy your Burrito Brunch.

Variation: Try using sandwich fillings or dinner leftovers in a tortilla to make a snack wrap.

UFO

Create this "unidentified frying object" for an all-in-one breakfast.

1. Using a small drinking cup, cut a hole out of the middle of a piece of bread.

2. Butter the bread on both sides and place it in a heated skillet.
3. Break an egg into the hole.
4. Cook the egg and bread for a few minutes on one side, then flip it over and cook the other side.
5. When the egg is done and the bread is lightly browned, serve your UFO on a plate.

Kamp Kabobs

With a stick and a few foods, you can turn just about anything into a Kamp Kabob.

1. Find a stick to use as a kabob skewer and clean it thoroughly.
2. Fill the skewer with any of the following: hot dog pieces, meatballs, ham cubes, pineapple, cherry tomatoes, bell pepper slices, or other meats, veggies and fruits.
3. Roast over the campfire until browned and sizzling.
4. Carefully remove to a plate and enjoy your kabobs.

Baked Eggs

You can cook your eggs right in the shells over hot coals.

1. Poke a small hole at the top of an egg, using a pin or other thin piece of metal.
2. Place the egg in hot ashes and bake for 20 minutes.
3. Carefully remove the egg and break it open over a piece of toast.

Tiger Teeth

This grinning snack is sure to bring smiles to your face.

1. Core an apple and slice it into 8 wedges to make 8 lips. (Each apple can make four tiger smiles.)
2. Spread peanut butter, cream cheese, or spreadable cheese on one side of each wedge to make gums.
3. Cut cheese into small cubes or use mini-marshmallows to make teeth.
4. Place a row of cheese teeth along one wedge and top it with another wedge, to make the Tiger Teeth. Repeat for remaining wedges.
5. Eat with a smile.

Edible Necklace

Instead of eating your cereal with milk, turn the cereal into a necklace and nibble it throughout the day.

1. Cut a piece of string or yarn long enough to make a necklace.
2. Fill the string with cereal that has holes in it, such as Cheerios, Fruit Loops, and so on.
3. Tie off the ends to complete the necklace.
4. Put on the necklace and munch on the cereal when you get hungry.

8

Gather Together for Fun!

Great Group Games and Activities

You'll probably be kept busy with lots of games and activities at camp, but once in a while you'll find time for some fast fun that doesn't take much preparation or have a lot of rules.

Games! Games! Games!

Here are some simple games and activities you can teach your camp mates whenever you get a break.

Tummy Ache

You'll need at least three friends and some floor space for this laugh-out-loud activity:

1. Lie down on your back with your head on another kid's tummy.
2. Have that kid put his head on the third person's tummy.
3. Continue until everyone is lying down in a circle with his head on another player's tummy.
4. Start the game by saying one "Ha!" out loud.
5. Have the second player say "Ha, ha" twice, the third player say "Ha, ha, ha" three times, and so on for each player.
6. You probably won't make it through every player, of course. After the first "Ha" or "Ha, ha," you'll all break into uncontrollable laughter, as your heads bob up and down like yo-yos on one another's bouncing tummies!

Quicksand!

When you're outdoors with some time on your hands, play a game of Quicksand and try not to fall into the hot molten lava. Here's what you do:

1. Play follow the leader and jump or leap from rock to log to stump to stone without falling or stepping onto the ground (quicksand!).
2. Eliminate each player who falls into the hot lava.
3. Keep going until there's only one player standing in safety.

Flashlight Tag

This is a great game for nighttime. Just be sure to get permission from your counselors before you play in the dark:

1. Choose one person to be the Big Game Hunter—the rest of the players are wild animals.
2. Each player takes a flashlight.
3. While the animals run and hide with their flashlights on, the Hunter tries to find them with his own flashlight.
4. The animals must keep moving so that the Hunter doesn't tag them with his flashlight beam. If he does, that animal is out—or becomes the Big Game Hunter.
5. Here's a trick: Shine the light in the Big Game Hunter's face so he can't easily tell where your light is coming from.

Hike Hunt

Play this game while you're out taking a hike:

1. Make a list of nature items to find along your hike, such as a smooth rock, jagged rock, acorn, dead bug, yellow leaf, piece of litter, flower, feather, seed pod, and so on.
2. Divide into teams or play individually and see who can find the most items on the list by the end of the hike.

"I sent along a small net, some small sealable plastic baggies, a bug catcher, and a fishing tackle box with lots of small dividers so my son could start a collection and have some places to store the objects he found."
—*Christy K.*

Winker

You and your friends can play this game at chow time without making a sound:

1. Get a deck of cards and count out enough black cards for each player—minus 1. If you have eight players, count out seven black cards.

2. Add one red card to the pile and put the rest of the cards aside.

3. Mix up the cards and pass them out to the players at the table.

4. Have them look at their cards without showing them to anyone else.

5. The person with the red card is the Winker. He must try to wink at all the other players in the game—one at a time—without being caught by any of the other players. That means he has to be quick, sly, and nonchalant when he gives another player a wink.

6. When a player is given a wink by the Winker, that player must wait a few seconds, then say "I'm out!" (He doesn't want to say it too soon because it might give away who the Winker is.)

7. If the Winker can wink at all the players before being caught, he wins the game. If he is caught winking at someone else by another player before he has winked at everyone, he loses.

8. Reshuffle the cards and pass them out again for a new game. And don't forget to eat your food while you play!

Nature Golf

Create a makeshift game of golf using items found in nature:

1. Find some sticks to use as golf clubs.
2. Designate tree trunks, logs, or stones to serve as the "holes."
3. Find some round oak balls, acorns, or small pinecones to use as golf balls, then try to hit the "balls" with the "clubs" to the "holes."

Bug Race

Make your own racetrack and find a few critters to cross the finish line:

1. Locate a patch of dirt and draw a track about three feet long, using a stick to mark the lanes.
2. Draw a starting line and a finish line with the stick at the top and the bottom of the track.
3. Search the bushes for some bugs to race, such as caterpillars, ladybugs, snails, and so on. Be careful not to find any snakes!

4. Line them up at the starting line and watch them go.
5. See which one crosses the finish line—or at least comes close.

Sock Scramble

This can be a stinky game—but that's half the fun:

1. Gather your camp mates' socks and hide them all around the camp site.
2. Tell your friends you've hidden their socks and they have to search the camp to find them.
3. Whoever finds both their socks first wins the game.
4. Play the game with the campers' underwear, if you dare.

Bug Hunt

How many bugs can you find in camp?

1. Give each player a pencil and paper.
2. Have them race to search the area for as many different bugs as they can find in a 20-minute period.
3. Instead of collecting the bugs, have the players write the names of the bugs, give descriptions, or do drawings on the paper.
4. Gather together and count up your list to see who found the most critters.

Touch and Tell

Can you tell what it is just by touch?

1. Collect a number of interesting nature items, including a live bug or two.
2. Put them in separate paper bags.
3. Pass them around the circle of camp mates.
4. Have them reach into the bag and feel each item, then try to guess what it is. Tell them not to say anything out loud until everyone has had a turn to touch the object.
5. When everyone has guessed, pull the object out of the bag and see how many people guessed correctly.

Franken-plant

Make your own new species of plant life:

1. Gather a variety of plant parts, including flower petals, leaves, stems, and so on.
2. Place the items on a table.
3. Pass out sheets of white construction paper.

"Stick a small bottle of calamine lotion into the first aid kit so your child can use it if he thinks he's contacted poison oak. If used early, it can help prevent spreading. I also included some non-stinging Bactine to help relieve the pain and itch of insect bites. My daughter was covered with bites, and topical anesthetic really helped her sleep at night."   —*Candy N.*

4. Separate the plant parts and reconstruct a whole new species of plant on your paper by creatively gluing the pieces into place.

5. Show off your new plants, give them a name, and see how unique and imaginative each one is.

Hunter!

See if you can make the other players move when they're not supposed to:

1. Call out "bird" and have the players raise themselves up as high as they can.

2. Then call out "snake" and have players squat down as far as possible.

3. Keep calling out "bird" and "snake" until you finally say "hunter!"

4. Everyone must freeze in midmovement.

5. If a player moves, he's out of the game.

Litter Hunt

Play a game that's not only fun but benefits the campsite and nature, too:

1. Give each player a paper bag.

2. Have them collect as much litter as they can find in 20 minutes.

3. Gather together when time is up and see who collected the most litter.

Story Sounds

Can you tell a story using sounds?

1. The leader makes a sound with his body, such as rubbing hands, tapping knees, slapping thighs, clicking fingers, and so on.

2. The next person begins telling a story that incorporates the sound. For example, if the first player makes a whooshing sound, the second player might begin the story like this: "One dark night there came the sound of the wind at the door . . ."

3. The second player makes a sound, and the next player must use that sound as he continues the story.

4. Keep going until everyone has had a turn or two and the story comes to an end.

Scary Stories

Telling ghost stories is a tradition at most campfires. There's something about gathering around the flames—in the dark, in the middle of the woods—that's all part of the camping experience. The trick is not to get so scared that you can't get to sleep after the stories are over! The first thing to remember is this: The stories were created to scare you. They're not real, no matter how much the storyteller—or your camp mates—say they are. They're called "urban legends," or, in this case, "camp legends," and they've been passed around for years and years. No doubt the stories you hear at the campfire will be the same stories your parents heard when they were kids because they're good stories. Now that you know the truth about scary stories, here's one you can share with your camp mates. It even has "body parts" to go with the story. It takes a little preparation, but it's worth it. Here's the story:

Mystery of the Missing Body Parts

"Once upon a time, there was this kid who didn't want to go to camp. He was afraid of the evil camp counselor, who was rumored to have special powers. The rumor was, if the camp counselor didn't like something you did, he would cause one of your body parts to drop off, just like that! Here's what they say happened to the camp kid.

The first day at camp, the counselor asked the kid to stir the pot of boiling potatoes, but the kid refused because he wanted to go play ball. That night he went to sleep, and when he woke up, he found his finger lying next to him in his sleeping bag! (At this point, pass around a paper bag that contains

a carrot about the size of a finger. Have the kids feel what's inside the bag without looking at it.)

The second day, the counselor asked the kid to eat all his dinner, but the kid refused because he didn't like what they were serving. That night he went to sleep, and when he woke up, he found his teeth had fallen out during the night! (Pass around a paper bag with some popcorn kernels that feel like teeth.)

The third day, the counselor asked the kid to tell the rest of the kids to come to campfire, but the kid refused and talked back to the counselor. That night he went to sleep, and when he woke up, he found his tongue had fallen out! (Pass around a bag with an apricot half inside.)

The fourth day, the counselor asked the kid to help him cook the dinner, but the kid refused and lied about having a tummy ache. That night he went to sleep, and when he woke up, he found his guts had fallen out! (Pass around a bag of cooked macaroni.)

The fifth day, the counselor asked the kid to watch out for wild animals during the campfire, but the kid refused because he wanted to read comic books. That night he went to sleep, and when he woke up, he found his eyes had fallen out! (Pass around a bag with two peeled grapes.)

The sixth day, the counselor asked the kid to help plan a game for the others, but the kid refused and lied about having a headache. That night he went to sleep, and when he woke up, he found his brains had fallen out! (Pass around a bag of cooked spaghetti.)

The seventh day, the counselor asked the kid to help take care of a sick camper, but the kid refused because he didn't like the sick kid. That night he went to sleep, and when he woke up, he found his heart—still beating—on the floor next to him! (Pass around a bag with a peeled tomato.)

And when he didn't come to breakfast that morning, the counselors went to his tent. But he had disappeared! All that was left were his body parts!"

(Prepare the foods ahead of time, put them in bags, and have them ready to pass around during the story. You can substitute other foods or objects that are similar to the body parts mentioned if you prefer.)

Put on a Skit

You can really cut loose at camp by acting in a silly skit and getting a few laughs from the audience. Sometimes the camp counselors have short plays you can do, but you can also create your own skits easily with a few of the following suggestions:

1. Choose a favorite book that everyone knows, such as *Red Riding Hood, Three Little Pigs,* or *Harry Potter.*
2. Rewrite the story to make it funny or related to camp. For example, if you choose *Red Riding Hood,* make Red a bear instead of a girl and turn the three bears into three campers. Then have the bear go after the campers' sleeping bags, backpacks, and camp food.
3. Assign roles, tell the actors to use funny accents while playing the parts, and take it from there!

9

Make It Yourself

Camp Arts and Crafts

Y ou'll probably have the opportunity to do some arts and crafts at camp, but if you'd like to do more, here are some crafts you can make on your own, with easy-to-find materials and simple-to-follow instructions.

Nature Crafts

The out-of-doors provides lots of materials for making things, so use what's available to you at your camp. Just make sure you have permission to take and use the nature items since some may be endangered or off limits to you.

Pressed Flowers and Leaves

Pressing flowers and leaves is a fun way to turn nature items into decorative objects:

1. Collect some pretty wild flowers or interesting leaves—or both—from around the camp. (Watch out for poison oak and poison ivy, though.)
2. Carefully place them inside a book, spreading out each individual petal or leaf. If you don't have a book, anything heavy and flat will do.
3. Allow the flowers and leaves to flatten for a day or two.
4. When they're ready, use them to decorate your journal, scrapbook, letters home, picture frames, and so on. You can either glue them on with white glue or use clear tape and cover them completely.

Twig Creatures

Make your own monsters out of dried and broken twigs, allowing the shape to guide your imagination:

1. Collect some short twigs and branches from the ground.

"Buy some popsicle sticks and pipe cleaners and stuff them in the bag. They're great for creating all kinds of things. We made a dinosaur skeleton out of them and buried them in the dirt for other kids to find them. Then we had to try to put the dinosaur together like a puzzle."
—*Melody J.*

2. Assemble them together into strange alien creatures by tying them together with thread or string or by gluing them and allowing the glue to set.

3. Add facial details with black or colored markers, such as one eye, some sharp teeth, four noses, and so on.

4. Display the creatures in your tent to protect you against nighttime creatures or give them to friends as a memento of camp.

5. For more fun, add leaves, flowers, acorns, pinecones, feathers, and other nature items to give the creatures more detail.

Camp Cabin

Create a reproduction of your camp cabin so you'll remember all the fun you had when you get home:

1. Gather some twigs from around the camp, all about the same thickness.

2. Break the twigs so they're all the same length.

3. Build the cabin by laying down two twigs parallel to each other.

4. Lay down two more twigs perpendicular to the first two to form a square. Overlap the ends and tie them together with thread or string or connect them with glue.

5. Continue to add layers of twigs, two at a time, until you've got a good-sized cabin.

6. Allow the twigs to dry if you're using glue.

7. When dry, add a roof by laying twigs over the top of the cabin.

8. Draw the cabin details, such as windows, doors, door-knobs, and the name of the cabin, using black markers.

9. If you have time and interest, build and set up the whole camp!

Flower Necklace

Make your own beautiful flower necklaces for yourself and your new friends:

1. Pick some daisies or other wildflowers with long stems, about 2 inches in length.

2. Using your thumbnail, make a slit near the bottom of the stem—right in the middle and long enough to insert another flower stem. Be careful not to make the slit too big or too long, or it may break.

3. Insert a flower stem into the slit and pull it through until the flower reaches the slit.

4. Insert another flower stem into the next slit and repeat until your flower chain is long enough to make a necklace and fit over your head.

5. Wear your new necklace while you make more for your friends.

Pinecone Picture Holder

If you've brought pictures from home or have taken snapshots of your new friends, here's a great way to display them—at camp and back home:

1. Find a large pinecone with a flat bottom.
2. Brush off the dirt and remove any sap.
3. Set the pinecone on a shelf or ledge (use some clay to keep it steady if it wiggles).
4. Insert pictures around the pinecone, using the stiff leaves to hold them in place. Rotate the pinecone now and then to show off different pictures.

Images of Nature

If you don't think you're a good artist, use this method to re-create images of nature and bring home some beautiful camp memories:

1. Get a sheet of white paper and a crayon.
2. Find something flat in nature that you would like to reproduce on paper, such as a large leaf, a feather, a flower, a snakeskin, a fossil, or an animal track.
3. Peel the paper off the crayon and lay the paper over the object.
4. Gently but firmly rub the side of the crayon over the object. The image should begin to appear on the paper.
5. Save the picture, and when you get home, you can frame it. Or cut out the image and use it to decorate your journal, scrapbook, or letters home.

Blade Blower

Make your own music with only a blade of grass as your instrument:

1. Pick a wide grass blade, a little longer than your thumb.
2. Hold your thumbs together, side by side.
3. Place the blade between your thumbs, securing it tightly at the top and bottom of your thumbs. There should be a small space between your thumbs.
4. Hold your thumbs up to your mouth and blow into the space where the blade is. You should hear a really interesting sound.
5. If you have trouble, adjust the grass blade and your thumbs until you're able to create the noise. It may take a little practice.
6. Have several of your friends make Blade Blowers, then hum some songs while you blow your blades.

Potpourri

Bring the scent of nature home to help remind you of that fresh outdoor smell. (And stick some potpourri in your soiled sock bag while you're at camp, too.):

1. Gather some nature items that have a pleasant scent, such as flower blossoms, tiny pinecones, dried moss, holly berries, pine sprigs, spruce leaves, pine needles, and so on.
2. Collect the items in a bag, then sort through them to make sure each item has a nice smell. Discard anything that you don't like. You never know when something might be sprayed by a skunk.

3. Break the items into little pieces and place them in a clean sock. Tie off the top in a knot to keep the potpourri inside.

4. Place the potpourri sock in your suitcase to help your clothes smell nice, then put it in your underwear drawer when you get home to remind you of the fragrant smell of nature.

Arty Crafts

You'll need a few arts and crafts supplies to make these creative and decorative objects, so check with your camp counselor for materials.

Buddy Bracelet

Work with a friend to make these Buddy Bracelets, then exchange them as a sign of your friendship:

1. Cut six 24-inch strands of embroidery thread.
2. Hold the strands together with the ends matched up, then tie an overhand knot 1 inch from an end.

3. Tape the knot to a tabletop.
4. Holding the free end, twist the bunch repeatedly in the same direction until it is tightly wound.
5. Pinch the twisted band in the center and fold it in half so that the free end matches up with the knotted end.
6. Release the center, and the band will automatically twist back on itself.
7. Slip the ends through the loop at the opposite end of the band, tie a knot to secure the bracelet, knot again, and trim the ends.
8. Measure the bracelet as you work to make sure it's long enough to fit around your wrist.
9. When the bracelet is finished, tie it onto your new friend's wrist with a triple knot and cut the excess string.
10. Wear your bracelets the whole time you're at camp and as a memento of your friend when you get home.
11. You can also braid some embroidery floss or string some beads to make a simple Buddy Bracelet.

"I bought some small craft kits at the toy store and put them in the suitcase as a surprise for my daughter. Things like jewelry-making kits, bead kits, braiding kits, and embroidery kits. She shared them with the other girls in her tent, and they used them when there was nothing else to do. Thanks to those kits, she said she was never bored." —*Deb B.*

Mystery Masterpiece

You'll need some friends to help you with this mysterious picture. Then watch what develops:

1. On a sheet of white paper, draw a wiggly line or shape with a colored marker.
2. Pass the paper to the next camper and have him add another line or shape, using a different colored marker.
3. Keep passing the paper around, adding more lines and shapes, until everyone has had a turn.
4. Hold the picture up for all to see and have everyone write down what they think it is by giving it a name, such as "Bird in Flight" or "Camp at Sunset."
5. See how many campers see the same image in the picture.
6. Repeat, starting with a different camper each time.

Camp Memory Book

Make a memory book of your adventures at camp and add to it each day. Then look it over when you get home and share stories of your adventures with your friends and family:

1. Get some colored construction paper, enough sheets for each day that you're going to be at camp, plus a couple extras for the front and back.
2. Punch or poke holes along one side of the papers.
3. Tie the papers together with yarn or string to make a book.
4. Collect items related to camp each day, such as leaves or feathers, lunch and dinner menus, daily activities, letters

from home or friends, camp crafts, drawings, snapshots, and so on.

5. On the first page, write "Welcome to Camp (fill in name)" or other greeting.

6. On the second page, write "Day 1 at Camp (fill in name)."

7. Lay out the items you want to include in the memory book so you have an interesting design. Fill both pages if you like.

8. Glue or tape the items onto the pages.

9. Add captions to each item using colored markers, such as "This is my new friend, Rebecca" or "Lunch is served!"

10. On the last page, get autographs from all your new camp friends.

Flying Squirrel

Make a flying squirrel and send it soaring through the trees:

1. Fold a brown sheet of construction paper in half lengthwise (or use white paper and color it brown).

2. Fold over each side again, the opposite direction.

3. Fold over each side again, the same direction.

4. Draw details of the squirrel on the outside, including eyes, nose, mouth, ears, and feet.

5. Now soar your flying squirrel to the tops of the trees.

6. See who can fly his squirrel the highest or the farthest. (You can also make a variety of birds.)

Soap Carving

Do some whittling using a bar of soap to make shower time a little more fun:

1. Draw a shape on a bar of soap, using a pencil or nail file. You might draw a plump bird, a fat snake, a big acorn, and so on.
2. Using a camp knife, nail file, or paring knife (with permission), begin to cut away pieces of the soap that are not part of the shape.
3. When you've got a rough version of the shape, use the knife or file to fine-tune the edges and make the details of the shape.
4. Use your special soap to get clean each day.

Stone People

See what it might be like to camp during the Stone Age with these Stone People as your camp mates:

1. Find some smooth stones to use as your characters.
2. Draw creative characters on the stones using black markers. You might want to make monsters, wild animals, caricatures of your camp mates or counselors, or cartoon characters.
3. Fill in details with paint or colored markers. Include their faces, bodies, arms, and legs.
4. Give each one a name and set them up along a shelf or window ledge.

Wacky Awards

Start making plans for Wacky Awards to hand out to all the campers on the last night of camp. You and your camp mates can design the awards on sheets of paper or on rocks and stones and decorate them with colored markers. On the last night, pass them out at a special ceremony during the final campfire gathering. Make sure the awards are fun, not mean, so you don't hurt anyone's feelings. Here are some suggestions for Wacky Awards:

"Loudest Snorer"   "Dirtiest Clothes"
"Best Table Manners"   "Most Creative Hat"
"Weirdest Walk"   "Biggest Eater"
"Nicest Smile"   "Pickiest Eater"
"Most Freckles"   "Wildest Laugh"
"Biggest Bed Hog"   "Strangest Sneezer"
"Silliest Slippers"   "Fastest Talker"
"Longest Showerer"   "Cleanest Nails"
"Coldest Hands"

10

Into the Wilderness

Nature Know-How

While you're out in nature, you'll need to know what to take, what to watch for, and how to keep safe. Here are some things to keep in mind.

Take a Hike

When it's time to take a hike, here are a few tips to help prepare you.

What to Take

While you're packing up your backpack for your upcoming hike, don't forget to bring the following:

- Backpack: to put everything in
- Band-Aids: in case you cut yourself or get a scrape
- Water bottle: for when you get thirsty
- Garbage bag: to keep your trash in
- Tissues or wet wipes: to clean off dirt, wash off possible poison oak, or cool yourself off
- Sunscreen: so you don't get sunburned
- Notebook and pencil: for notes and observations
- Insect repellent: to keep the bugs off
- Knife: if allowed, to cut your path
- Compass: so you know which way you're going and how to get back

What to Wear

In order to stay comfortable on the hike, consider wearing or taking the following:

- Comfortable hiking shoes: so your feet won't hurt
- Long pants: so you won't get poison oak or scratched-up legs
- Long T-shirt: to protect you from the sun and the brambles
- Socks: to collect all those stickers you get to pull out when you get back to camp
- Hat: to look cool, keep cool, and avoid sunstroke
- Bandanna: to keep the sweat off your neck

What to Know

Here are the rules of the trail to keep in mind along the way:

- No littering: so the trail doesn't fill up with garbage
- Get permission before trespassing: so you don't get arrested, in trouble, or stuck where you can't get out
- Don't remove nature items: unless you have permission; otherwise, there won't be any nature left
- Stick to the trail: so you don't get lost or fall down a cliff
- Get home before dark: so you don't have to spend a cold night on the trail, in the dark, all night
- Stay with a friend: so the two of you can figure out how to solve any problems that arise, and you don't get lonely

What to Watch For

Here are some things to look for while you're on your hike:

- Animal tracks: Try to identify the tracks and which animals they belong to.
- Animal homes: Look for habitats, such as caves, holes, trees, and other places where animals live.
- Birds' nests: Check the trees and bushes and creeks for birds' nests and try to figure out which birds belong to which nests.
- Eggs: Look in the nests for eggs, but be careful not to touch them.
- Pellets: Also known as horse apples, cow pies, bat guano, and other variations on animal doo-doo—try not to step in any.

- Rocks: Scan the rocks you come across and see how many variations you can identify.
- Plants: Bring along a guide book and name as many plants as you can.
- Birds: Look up in the sky and see if you can spot all different kinds of birds.
- Bugs: Look down at the ground and see if you can spot all different kinds of bugs and insects.

What to Watch Out For

Just like anywhere, there are dangers on the trail, so watch out for the following:

- Poison plants: Watch for poison oak, poison ivy, and poison sumac. Learn how to identify poisonous plants and steer clear of them so you don't break out in an itchy rash. If you do think you've made contact with a poisonous plant, see the camp nurse immediately.
- Getting lost: Mark your trail as you go so you don't get lost. Tie pieces of string, lay down twigs, or set up stones to remind you which way you came and how to get back. Stay on the path and keep with your group at all times.
- Wild animals: There's safety in numbers, so stay with your group. If you think you see a bear, either freeze, climb a tree, or run like crazy. Most likely they're

Aiece!!

more afraid of you than you are of them. But don't take any chances.

On the Trail

Besides enjoying the fresh air, great exercise, and new surroundings, there are lots of other fun things to do along the trail.

Tracking the Trail

See if your trail buddies can follow your trail by watching for directions along the way. Divide into two groups. One group hikes the trail first, leaving markers on the trail. The other group follows a few minutes later, interpreting the instructions along the path. Here are some ways to indicate your direction as you go:

Go straight = line three rocks up in a row or make the sign of an arrow using three twigs.

Turn left = line up two rocks, put one rock on the left, or lay out two sticks, one pointing straight, one pointing left.

Turn right = line up two rocks, put one rock on the right, or lay out two sticks, one pointing straight, one pointing right.

Turn around = line up rocks in an upside-down U shape or place three twigs in an upside-down U.

Turn right at the tree = tie a string or scrap of cloth on the right side of a tree.

Turn left at the tree = tie a string or scrap of cloth on the left side of the tree.

Cross the creek = lay down a twig and make a line of rocks going over the twig.

Watch out—danger ahead! = three rocks stacked on one another.

Follow the Map

Direct the hikers on a map-reading expedition and see if they make it to their destination:

1. Divide into two groups.
2. The first group takes a sheet of paper and pencil on the trail and draws a map of the route as they go.
3. Put in landmarks along the way, such as large rocks, fallen trees, creek beds, caves, fence posts, and so on.
4. In the meantime, the second group does the same, using a different path.
5. Bring the maps back to camp, exchange them, and see how well each group does by following the map.

Night Hike

Ask your camp counselors to take you on a night hike, using your flashlights to light your way:

1. Have one serve as leader and one at the back to make sure everyone stays safe.
2. Stay on the path, hike slowly, and use extra caution in the dark.

3. See if you can find the North Star, then keep an eye on the stars so you know which direction you're going. A night hike is kind of scary, but it's also exciting and fun.

Blind Walk

While you're out hiking, take a few minutes for a Blind Walk:

1. Find a partner you can trust.
2. Have him lead you along the path while you keep your eyes closed.
3. Your partner should tell you when there are dangers in the path, including low-hanging trees, dips and obstacles along the way, and other things to watch out for.
4. You can either hold on to your partner's hand or just listen to his voice and use it as your guide.
5. Take turns leading each other—and make sure you keep the trust.

Nature Scavenger Hunt

There are so many things to look for on a Nature Scavenger Hunt:

1. Ask your camp counselor to make a list of nature items to collect.
2. Break into teams and race to see who can find the most items.
3. When you get back to camp, use the items to make a collage to take home at the end of camp.

Dinosaur Bones

They're not exactly "dinosaur" bones, but they'll do. Besides, your camp mates will have a lot of fun reconstructing the "dinosaur":

1. Ask the kitchen if they have any clean chicken bones. If they're not clean, ask the cook to boil them in water to clean them, then come back later to collect them.
2. Find an area where you can bury the bones and dig up a couple of inches of dirt.
3. Break apart the bones at the joints, lay them in the dirt, and cover them up.
4. Tell your friends you found some bones—possibly a dinosaur skeleton—and get them to help you dig them up.
5. Try to piece the bones together like a puzzle.
6. Name your discovery after the camp, such as Campalosifus or Tyrannacampus Rex.

Birdseed Pinecone Feeders

While you're at camp, create a bird feeder so you can watch the birds up close as they eat:

1. Ask the camp cook for some peanut butter and seeds or cereal bits.
2. Find a pinecone and tie a string to the top of the pinecone.

3. Spread some peanut butter on the pinecone and sprinkle on some seeds or cereal bits.
4. Tie the pinecone to a tree and invite the birds to dinner.

Star Search

Spend some time under the night sky and see what you can see:

1. Bring your flashlight and a chart of the night sky constellations.
2. Lie down under the stars with your camp mates and see how many constellations you can find.
3. Take turns creating your own con-stellations, using the stars as your guide, and see if you can spot a boat, a house, a bicycle, a dinosaur, and so on.

 Tip

To keep burrs and stickers from your shoes, rub a little wax or soap on them.

Nature Collections

Start a collection of nature items while you're at camp and see how many you can find before you leave. Here are some suggestions for collections:

Bird feathers
Animal tracks (drawings or rubbings)
Leaves (except poisonous ones!)
Layers of dirt (place in a jar)
Nuts and berries
Flowers
Rocks

Litter

Animal sounds (recorded)

Unusual nature items

Follow the Floater

How far will your floater travel before it sinks?

1. Find something from nature that will float, such as a large leaf, a twig, a pinecone, a feather, and so on.
2. Mark the object with a black marker or red lipstick so you can identify it as it travels.
3. Head for a nearby creek with a buddy and take along your floaters.
4. Place your floaters in the creek and see how far you can follow them as they float downstream.
5. Repeat with a new floater and see if it goes farther each time.

Rock City

Build a miniature city using rocks and stones and see how elaborate you can make it:

1. Gather some rocks and stones from the area.
2. Use the rocks to create a structure, such as a city, a house, a campsite, or a maze.
3. Add to your structure each day, making it bigger and more complex each time.
4. Take a picture when it's finished to show your family when you get home.

Blazing a Trail

Can your friends follow the trail you've blazed through the wilderness? Try this and see:

1. Find a wide stick, about as long as your legs.
2. Gather some friends and head for a dirt path.
3. Tell your friends to wait five minutes before following you, then head off along the path, dragging the stick behind you.
4. As you go off in different directions, make sure your stick leaves a trail along the ground that your friends can follow.
5. See if you can return to the start before your friends catch up with you on the path.
6. Take turns leaving a trail for each other.

Pinecone Critters

Use your imagination to create a creepy critter out of prickly pinecones:

1. Gather some pinecones, along with other small nature items, such as feathers, leaves, twigs, stems, flowers, berries, nuts, seeds, and so on.
2. Set the pinecone on its side or upright, depending on how you want your critter to look.
3. Glue the small nature items into the pinecone to form legs, arms, head, antennae, eyes, mouth, nose, and so on to make an interesting critter.
4. Make as many critters as you like, then give them to friends or keep them to take home.

11

Wish You Were Here

Letters to Home

Your family and friends will miss you while you're at camp having all that fun. So the one thing you can do for them is write letters and keep them informed and entertained. Sometimes writing letters seems like a chore—after all, you're having too much fun to write. But you can turn it into a good time with a little creativity and imagination. Here are some ways to make your letters fun to write and fun to read.

"Dear Mom and Dad"

The most important people to write are your parents. After all, they're the ones who will miss you the most—and the ones who paid for camp! They're the most eager to hear how things are going and to find out if you're having a good time. Here are some suggestions for writing letters to mom and dad, sister or brother, grandmother and grandfather, and your friends.

Letter Prompts

If you need ideas for what to write, try using these letter prompts to get you started. Just choose the most appropriate words you need to get your thoughts across:

"Dear (Mom and Dad) (Sister or Brother) (Grandma and Grandpa) (Best Friend) (Old Pal):

Camp is (awesome) (great) (fun) (interesting) (weird) (a jungle).

I have met (lots of new friends) (one really cool kid) (a nice counselor) (the camp nurse) (a friendly bear).

The food is (just like home cooking) (not bad) (needs catsup) (tastes like cardboard) (must be cat food).

My favorite activities are (swimming) (hiking) (eating) (resting) (writing letters home).

I have learned lots of new things, like how to (tie a knot) (make a wallet) (shoot an arrow) (make my bed) (burp extra loud).

What I miss the most is (my family) (my friends) (my pets) (my bedroom) (my stuff).

When I get home I want to (give you a kiss and hug) (see my friends) (tease my sister/brother) (play with my cat/dog) (have a hamburger).

Thanks for sending me (letters) (pictures) (snacks) (toys) (money).

That's all for now. See you (soon) (sometime) (whenever) (who knows?) (actually, I'm not coming home).

Love (Bye Bye) (Later) (Sincerely yours) (Gotta go),

(Your name) (your camper kid) (your adorable son/daughter) (the joy of your life).

Who Else to Write To

You might really get into writing letters, so you'd better have a list of people to write. Here are some suggestions for people besides your parents:

- ◆ Sisters and brothers
- ◆ Grandparents
- ◆ Friends
- ◆ Neighbors
- ◆ Teachers
- ◆ Church leaders
- ◆ Pets
- ◆ Camp friends

Special Stationery

Make your letters more interesting by using creative paper and lettering. Here are some suggestions for fun letters:

- Cut out words or letters from newspapers and glue them onto the paper to make a ransom note. Say something like, "If you ever want to see your kid again, send chocolate chip cookies!"

- Write a letter on a roll of toilet paper, roll it up or fold it, and mail it to your sisters and brothers.

- Write your letter, then cut it up into jigsaw pieces and put it into an envelope so your family has to put it together to read it.

- Write your letter and add stains all over it, such as chocolate, dirt, food, lipstick, dead bug, and so on. Draw arrows to the stains and make up stories to go with them or have your family try to guess what each stain is!

- Write your letter by drawing pictures to replace some of the words. For example, instead of writing "I love camp!" draw a picture of yourself, then a heart, then a picture of the camp or a tent.

- Write your letter on a piece of paper found at camp, such as the daily activity sheet or a piece of not-too-dirty trash.

"When I went to horse camp, mom bought me a brand new stationery set with red paper and heart stickers. I was afraid of the horses so I stayed in the camp and wrote a lot of letters. Everyone in camp loved my stationery. She also sent a bunch of teen magazines for everyone to read, full of cute guys in them. My mom knew I loved to do arts and crafts so she packed extra write T-shirts for me to tie-dye."

—*Sue W.*

◆ Write your letter on a paper you've decorated in arts and crafts class.

◆ Send postcards of camp with a short note on the back. Don't forget to include "Having a wonderful time. Wish you were here!"

◆ Draw a map of the camp and explain where everything is. Send that as your letter.

◆ Glue dried or pressed flowers to the letter or other items from nature or camp.

◆ Write your letter using fancy letters that look like bubbles, have shadows, use patterns, or are three-dimensional.

◆ Write part of your letter out of leaves and seeds, attached with glue.

◆ Write the letter in code (and send the code along with the letter so the reader can decode it!).

◆ Write the letter on white paper using a white crayon, then send a black crayon and tell the reader to color the paper with the black crayon in order to read the message.

◆ Use fun abbreviations in your letter, such as the following:

SUP (What's up?)

LOL (Laughing out loud)

ROFL (Rolling on the floor laughing)

OTQT (On the quiet/ keep it secret)

OMG (Oh my gosh!)

JK (Just kidding)

BTW (By the way)

B4N (Bye for now)

CUL8R (See you later)

TT4N (Ta-ta for now)

TTYL (Talk to you later)

IMU (I miss you)

G2G (Got to go)

L8R (Later)

TMW (Tomorrow)

X & O (Kisses and hugs)

LYL (Love ya lots)

 Tip

If you can't think of anything to write about, make up a long, completely wild adventure— and then write "P.S. Just kidding!"

- ◆ Write a "to be continued" letter, stop in the middle of a sentence, and mail a new letter continuing the story each day.

- ◆ Write the whole letter in a spiraling circle or other design so the reader has to keep turning the paper to read the message.

- ◆ Sign the letter with a funny fake name, such as Aida Bugg, Nita Bath, Ima Kidder, Olive Yew, or U. R. Knotty.

- ◆ Decorate the envelope with drawings of camp or use fancy letters to write the name and address. Just make sure it's still readable!

Things to Write About If You Can't Think of Anything

Here are some suggestions for subjects to write if you've run out of ideas:

◆ Your tent or cabin: what it looks like, what you like about it, what you don't like about it

◆ Your tent mates: their personalities, what they brought, what they do that makes you laugh, where they're from, how they're enjoying camp

◆ Your camp counselors: your favorites, your not-so-favorites, what they do at camp, where they're from, what's funny about them

◆ The food: the food you like, what you don't like, a food you couldn't identify, a food you tried that you've never had before, something you did with the food for fun, what you miss eating the most, what you never hope to eat again

◆ The animals: what you've seen, what you've heard is there but haven't spotted yet, what you hope to see, the noises you hear at night, how your pets would do at camp, signs of animals you've found, animal habitats (homes), your favorite animal

◆ Nature: something in nature you learned more about, any poisonous plants you've spotted, what you've made from nature, your favorite part of nature, what you still hope to see

◆ Activities: your favorite activities, an activity you hope to do, an activity you wish they had but don't, an activity you're good at, something you made that you're bringing home, something you want to do when you get home that you learned at camp

◆ Jokes and pranks: something funny you did, something funny someone did to you, what you hope to do next, your most embarrassing moment, anything you got in trouble for, a joke you played against a counselor

◆ Miscellaneous: the weather, the camp facilities, the ride to camp, what you miss the most about home, what you like most about camp, what you're going to do when you get home, any dreams you've had, the funniest thing about camp, what you'll miss the most about camp

12

Dear Diary . . .

Filling Your Journal Pages

The time goes by so quickly at camp and there's so much to do, you don't want to forget a thing when you get back home. The best way to preserve those memories is by keeping a journal while you're at camp. All you need is a blank book or some paper and a pen. Here are some things you might want to include in your journal.

Daily Entries

At the end of each day, think about the highlights and jot them down in your journal. You can write as if you're writing a letter to someone special or write in note or list form and keep it simple. If you have trouble remembering everything that happened that day, break it down into four time periods:

Before breakfast or early morning (7 A.M. to 9 A.M.)
After breakfast or late morning (9 A.M. to noon)
After lunch or afternoon (noon to 5 P.M.)
After dinner or evening/night (5 P.M. to bedtime)

Special Events

You might want to include just the special events that occur at camp, such as daily activities, interesting adventures, evening campfires, and occasional outings. Save room for the first day and the last day especially since those are the most exciting days, filled with lots of activities and events.

Unforgettable Moments

You'll want to include all the unforgettable moments that occur at camp—and there will be plenty. A funny joke, the beginning of a new friendship, a tasty (or horrendous) meal, a special ceremony, a nature find, and so on. Keep your eyes and ears peeled so you don't miss anything important.

Things You May Have Forgotten

At the end of each journal entry, go over the day again and try to remember things that you may have overlooked, such as a special moment with a friend, a growth experience, something new that you learned, a feeling you had during a nature walk, your thoughts about camp or the future, and impressions you made each day.

These quiet, simple memories are just as important as the exciting activities and events that you jot down.

Fill-In Journal

Set aside a couple of pages at the beginning or end of the journal to record details and information for future reference. Write in the following prompts when you begin your journal, then fill them in as something occurs.

Tip

Swap e-mail addresses as well as street addresses; you may use both!

Camp Name. You don't want to forget the name of the camp in case you want to return next year. If the camp has a funny nickname, include that, too.

Group Name. Many camps assign group names or cabin names within the camp, so jot them down to help you remember them later. Write down the names of the campers in each group or cabin, too.

Friends' Names. Record all the new friends that you meet and include their nicknames or camp names as you learn them. Don't forget to add your own camp name if you get one.

Counselors' Names. Your counselors will be important to you, so write down their names as you learn them—both camp names or nicknames—so you don't forget them.

Addresses. Leave a page or two just for addresses of your new friends or counselors so you can write to them when you get back home and keep in touch over the next year until you return to camp.

Things I Love About Camp. Make a list of all the things you love about camp each day so you don't forget them. You might also make a list of the things you don't especially like about camp!

My Best Friend(s). You're sure to make one or more good friends at camp, so to help you remember them over the years, record some of the following information on a "Best Friends" page:

> Why my friend is cool:
> What I like best about my friend:
> One way I'd like to be like my friend:
> Fun things I did with my friend:
> Something I learned from my friend:
> How my friend is similar to me:
> How my friend is different from me:

Cutest Boy/Girl at Camp. Just in case you meet someone cute at camp, include some details in your journal or scrapbook so you can share the details with your friends. Describe him or her and maybe tell why you like him or her, then have a good giggle.

Pocketful of Memories: Place to Keep Your Keepsakes

You're likely to collect some mementos from camp, and you'll want to store them and keep them safe until you get home so you can show them to your friends and family and save them over the years. Here's an easy way to keep those loose mementos stored securely:

1. Make a pocket for your journal or scrapbook to keep your mementos safe.
2. Cut out a half sheet of paper.
3. Glue or tape the sides and bottom of the paper to a sheet of paper in your scrapbook or journal.
4. Stuff letters from home, snapshots, nature items, camp activity flyers, artwork, and other flat items inside the pocket.

13

Note to Campers

Safety and Basic First Aid

Y ou're going to have a great time at camp, but in order to ensure a wonderful adventure, you'll need to follow the rules—mother nature's *and* the camp's.

Stay Safe

There's no need to be afraid at camp—you'll be well protected. But it's a good idea to be cautious in order to stay safe in this new environment. Nature is a powerful force, and you need to respect it at all times. Here are some problems that may occur at camp and what you can do about them.

Heat Exhaustion

Symptoms: If it's very hot outdoors or you look pale or feel dazed, have cold and clammy skin, or feel faint, you may have heat exhaustion.

Remedy: Lie down in shady area, elevate your feet, loosen your clothes if they're tight, drink a little salted water, and call the camp doctor.

Prevention: Drink plenty of water, eat salty things, wear light clothing, and keep cool.

Sunstroke

Symptoms: If it's very hot outdoors and you have hot dry skin, feel dizzy, and have a rapid heartbeat, you may have sunstroke.

Remedy: Move to the shade, lie down, elevate your head, loosen any tight clothing, fan yourself, sponge yourself with cool water, and call your camp doctor.

Prevention: Stay out of the sun, wear a hat, drink plenty of water, and keep cool.

Scrapes and Cuts

Symptoms: You scrape yourself or get a cut and find that it's bleeding.

Remedy: Wash the area with soap and water if possible, coat it with antiseptic, and cover the area with a bandage. If it's serious, check with the camp doctor.

Prevention: Be careful.

Broken Bones and Sprains

Symptoms: If your arm or leg seems bent out of shape or is swollen or there's pain when you move it, you may have a broken bone or a sprain.

Remedy: Keep the injured area as still and comfortable as possible, apply an ice pack, and see the camp doctor.

Prevention: Be careful.

Shock

Symptoms: Shock is your body's automatic response to an injury. It slows down your bodily functions, makes your skin cold and clammy, and causes irregular breathing, a faint pulse, and quick heartbeat.

Remedy: Lie down, cover yourself up to prevent heat loss, and see your camp doctor.

Prevention: There's not much you can do to prevent shock except be careful so that you aren't injured, which is what causes the reaction.

Poison Oak, Ivy, Sumac

Symptoms: If you suspect you've come into contact with a poisonous plant, you may not experience any symptoms at first. In a day or two, the area may start burning or itching and become red and swollen, and blisters may form.

Remedy: Even if you suspect you may have come into contact with a poisonous plant, wash the area well with soap and water, then apply rubbing alcohol to the exposure. Change into clean clothes and keep the exposed clothing separate until it can be thoroughly washed or disposed of. If you get a rash, don't scratch it—keep the area dry, apply calamine lotion, keep the area cool, and see the camp doctor.

Prevention: Watch where you walk and what you touch.

Snake Bite

Symptoms: Most people live long and healthy lives after a snake bite, so don't panic. Watch for swelling in the bite area, some nausea, weakness, numbness, and possibly shock within two hours.

Remedy: Lie down, making sure the bitten area is lower than your heart, and put a snug band above the bite if it's on the arm or the leg. Get medical help, move slowly if you have to walk, and stay calm.

Identify the snake, if possible:

1. A rattlesnake is three to eight feet long, is found every-where, and sounds warning signals by rattling its tail.
2. A copperhead snake is usually three feet long, is found in hilly, rocky areas and in haystacks and barns, and has a camouflage color that helps it blend into ground and leaves.

3. A cottonmouth, or water moccasin, is about three to four feet long, is found in watery and swampy areas, and has a thick body with white inside the mouth.

4. A coral snake is about three feet long; is found burrowing in holes; and has colorful red, yellow, and white skin with a black swatch.

Prevention: Watch out for snakes and get a snakebite kit.

Ticks

Symptoms: Check your body for ticks.

Remedy: Remove the tick as soon as possible by covering the area with oil, then pull out the tick with tweezers. Wash the area with soap and water and use an antiseptic to prevent infection.

Prevention: Use insect repellent and stay out of areas where there are lots of ticks.

Spider Bites

Symptoms: Look for an area that's red, swollen, burning, or stinging, with some nausea or cramps.

Remedy: Tie a constricting band above the bite, then apply ice and see the camp doctor.

Prevention: Learn to identify poisonous spiders and avoid the black widow spider, which has a red hourglass-shaped mark on the belly; the brown recluse spider, which has a violin-shaped mark on its head and six eyes; and the tarantula, which is large and hairy.

Insect and Bee Stings

Symptoms: Ouch! You'll feel a painful sting.

Remedy: Remove the stinger by scraping it away, use ice on the area, and make a paste of baking soda or mud to soothe the sting.

Prevention: Watch out for bees, check to see if you are allergic to insect bites or bee stings, and get a bee sting kit.

Animal Bites

Symptoms: Teeth marks!

Remedy: Wash the wound with soap and water, cover the area with a bandage, and see your camp doctor.

Prevention: Avoid wild animals!

 Tip

To protect your feet from blisters, smear a bar of soap on the inside of your sock at the heel and toe areas.

Obey the Rules

One way to keep safe and enjoy the camp experience is to follow the rules laid out by the camp. Each camp has different rules, but all were designed for your safety so you'll leave camp with pleasant memories of a great experience. Follow *all* the rules—each one was created for a reason, even it's not clearly explained or doesn't make sense to you. Feel free to ask why a particular rule was made, if you're interested, but don't argue with your counselors. They know best. Most problems occur at camp when the rules are broken.

Report Problems to Camp Counselors

If you have a serious problem, get help. Don't try to solve everything yourself. The adults at camp have more experience than you and will help you find solutions to even the most serious problems. Don't be afraid to ask for assistance when you need it. If you feel homesick, suspect you're ill or in danger, have a problem with another camper, or *whatever* it might be, go to your immediate supervisor and let him or her know. If the counselor doesn't seem interested or take action, talk to another counselor or the camp director. Your general safety and well-being are of utmost concern to the people at camp.

Most counselors will keep your concerns confidential for your protection, so you don't need to worry about everyone finding out what's bothering you. Common problems you might need help with include dealing with a bully, nighttime fears or nightmares, bed-wetting, lack of friends, severe homesickness, and physical or emotional problems. Remember: They are there to help you with any problems or concerns you might have and are trained to work with kids.

Make the Most of the Experience

You're at camp to have a great time, so make the most of it. Explore the out-of-doors, the fun activities, the new friendships, and the whole camping experience. It may be the only time you have an adventure like this, and you'll want to enjoy every moment. The memories you make at camp will stay with you for a lifetime. And the moments are what you make of them. So have FUN!

Index

A

Abbreviations for letters, 185–186
ACA. *See* American Camping Association (ACA)
Activities. *See also* Arts and crafts; Fun and games; Trail activities
  for alone time, 39–40, 60
  arts and crafts, 158–169
  choosing a camp and, 6–7
  for overcoming homesickness, 39–40, 114–118
  specific versus general, 10
  trail activities, 170–180
  writing about, 188
Address book, 46, 57
Addresses, writing in journal, 192
Age
  ideal, for camp, 3
  maturity and, 4
Air travel safety tips, 96
Alphabet Adventure game, 97
American Camping Association (ACA)
  camp accreditation, 23–24
  safety measures recommended by, 25–26
  standards for camps, 24–25
Animal bites, 199
Animal Hunt game, 98
"Annoying Song," 76

"Ants Go Marching" song, 76–78
Anxieties. *See also* Homesickness; Safety issues; Separation from home and family
  fear of the dark, 38
  guilt about sending child to camp, 41
  safety concerns, 25–26
  severe homesickness signs, 42–43
  sharing feelings, 33
Apple Scramble, 141
Areas of interest, choosing a camp and, 6–7
Arts and crafts, 158–169
  arty crafts, 164–169
  Blade Blower, 163
  Buddy Bracelet, 164–165
  Camp Cabin, 160–161
  Camp Memory Book, 166–167
  Flower Necklace, 161
  Flying Squirrel, 167
  Images of Nature, 162
  Mystery Masterpiece, 166
  nature crafts, 158–164
  Pinecone Picture Holder, 162
  Potpourri, 163–164
  Pressed Flowers and Leaves, 159
  Soap Carving, 167–168
  stationery for letters, 183–185, 186

Arts and crafts *(continued)*
  Stone People, 168
  Twig Creatures, 159
  Wacky Awards, 168–169
Autograph book, 57
Awards, wacky, 168–169

B
"Baby Bumble Bee" song, 79
Backpack
  packing for camp, 56
  packing for hiking, 170–171
Backseat Bingo game, 98
"Backwards Song," 79
Baked Eggs, 144
Balloons, water, 75
Banana Boats, 140
Banana Chips, 70
Bandanna, 55
Banner, welcome home, 101–102
Bathrobe, 58
Bedding
  improvising, 68
  packing, 50
Bedroom makeover, 102
Bee stings, 199
"Be Kind to Your Fine-Feathered
    Friends" song, 80
Belly Button Art, 123
Benefits of camp, 34–35
"Best Friends" journal page, 192
"Bingo!" song, 80
Birdseed Pinecone Feeders, 177–178
Bird Watching Booklet, 104
Bites
  animal, 199
  insect and bee stings, 199
  snake, 187–188
  spider, 198–199
Black widow spider, 198–199
Blade Blower activity, 163
Blazing a Trail, 180
Blind Dots and Boxes, 132–133
Blind Walk activity, 176
Blisters, protecting feet from, 199
"Boa Constrictor" song, 81
Body Tattoos, 124
Bones, broken, 196

Books
  address book, 46, 57
  autograph book, 57
  Camp Memory Book, 166–167
  camp-related information, 105
  camp-themed stories, 64–67
  card-playing handbook, 61–62
  joke books, 60
  journal, 40–41, 61, 62, 116, 189–193
  Mad-Libs, 75
  of magic tricks, 61
  packing, 57, 63, 64–67
  puzzles and games, 61, 74
  scrapbook, 61, 62, 116
Boredom
  as cause of homesickness, 59, 114
  packing boredom busters, 39–40,
    59–62, 73–75
Bracelet, buddy, 164–165
Bribing, 41
Broken bones, 196
Brown recluse spider, 198–199
Buddy Bracelet, 164–165
Bug Hunt game, 151
Bug Race game, 150–151
Bugs on a Log, 143
Burrito Brunch, 143
Bus travel safety tips, 95–96

C
"Cabin in the Woods" song, 81
Camp Cabin activity, 160–161
Camp Characters, 126–127
Camp counselors. *See* Counselors
Camp director
  questions for, 26
  talking to, 26, 32, 42
Camp fairs, 22
Campfire songs. *See* Songs
Camp Memory Book, 166–167
"Camp Video Night," 35
Candy, packing, 52
Card games
  Crawlspace Concentration, 129
  Funny Fish, 128
  Mixed-Up Eights, 129
  packing, 61–62, 73
  Wacky War, 127–128

Card-playing handbook, 61–62
Card tricks, 130–131
Care packages, 40
Carry bag, 53
Car travel safety tips, 95
Celery sticks, 143
Chameleon Clothes gag, 138
Charades, 136
Chin Chum, 126
Choosing a camp, 3–27
    ACA accreditation and standards,
        23–26
    activities and areas of interest, 6–7
    child's involvement in, 32, 37
    determining readiness for camp, 4–5
    finding camps on the Web, 18–21
    goals of camp, 7–8
    kinds of camps available, 8–10
    overall philosophy of the camp, 6
    pros-and-cons list items, 11–12
    questions for the camp director, 26
    registering for camp, 27
    safety concerns, 25–26
    specific camps available, 13–18
Church, finding camps through, 22
Clothes
    awesome or favorite shirt, 58
    bathrobe, 58
    camp vest, 58
    for hiking, 171
    oversized t-shirts, 57
    packing, 51–52
    tank tops, 58
Clubs, finding camps through, 22
Code One game, 136–137
Cognitive skills learned at camp, 30
Collections, 61, 116, 148, 178–179
Colleges, finding camps through, 22
Colored pens. See Pens and markers
Communication. See Letters to camp;
        Letters to home; Talking
Compliments, for making friends, 112
Concentration, Crawlspace, 129
Confidence, learned at camp, 31
Cootie Catcher, 120–121
Copperhead snakes, 197–198
Coral snakes, 197–198
Costs of camps, 10

Cottonmouth snakes, 197–198
Counselors
    helping, 116–117
    reporting problems to, 200
Countdown calendar, 37
Counting Cars game, 98
Crafts. See Arts and crafts
Crawlspace Concentration game, 129
Crazy Eights card game, 129
Crunchy Trail Mix, 71
Cuts and scrapes, 195–196

D
Dark, fear of, 38
Day camps versus resident camps, 9
Decorations, welcome home, 103
Dinosaur Bones activity, 177
Dominoes, 136
Dots and Boxes, blind, 132–133
"Do Your Ears Hang Low?" song,
    81–82
Duffel bag, 53

E
Edible Necklace, 145
Eggs
    baked, 144
    Burrito Brunch, 143
    UFO (unidentified frying object),
        143–144
Eight-Legged Octopus, 142

F
Family, separation from. See Separa-
        tion from home and family
Family versus kids-only camps, 9–10
Favorite items, packing, 40
Fears. See Anxieties
Fifty States game, 98–99
Finding camps
    other methods, 21–22
    Web sites for, 18–21
First aid
    for animal bites, 199
    for broken bones and sprains, 196
    for heat exhaustion, 195
    for insect and bee stings, 199
    packing supplies for, 53–54, 152

First aid *(continued)*
  for poisonous plants, 173, 196–197
  for scrapes and cuts, 195–196
  for shock, 196
  for snake bite, 187–188
  for spider bites, 198–199
  for sunstroke, 195
  for ticks, 198
First Aid Guide, 104
First day at camp, 109–118
  making new friends, 111–114
  talking about homesickness,
    109–110
Fish card game, funny, 128
Flashlight
  keeping handy, 69
  packing, 54
  for séances, 134
  Shadow Shapes, 135
  Shooting Star, 135
  tag, 147
Flashlight Tag, 147
Flexible versus structured programs, 9
Flip-flops, 58
Flowers
  necklace, 161
  pressed, 159
Flying Squirrel activity, 167
Follow the Floater activity, 179
Follow the Map activity, 175
Food. *See also* Recipes
  campfire snacks, 139–145
  keeping away from critters, 69
  packaged snacks, 72–73
  recipes, 70–72
  trail mix, 63, 71–72
  treats and snacks, 69–73
  welcome home meal, 103
Forgotten items, dealing with, 63–64
Forms, packing, 54
Fortune Telling, 120–121
"Found a Peanut" song, 82–83
Four-Letter Words game, 133–134
Franken-plant game, 152–153
Freckle Face gag, 137
Friends
  being a good friend, 114
  "Best Friends" page in journal, 192
  finding camps through, 21

  as goal of camp, 7
  inviting to camp, 39
  making at camp, 7, 111–114
Frisbee Golf, 74
Fruit Leather, 70
Fun and games. *See also* Activities;
    Group games; Tent-time activi-
    ties; Travel entertainment
  for alone time, 39–40, 60
  boredom busters, 39–40, 59–62,
    73–75
  card games, 61–62, 73, 127–129
  card tricks, 130–131
  in the dark, 38
  flashlight fun, 134–135
  Frisbee Golf, 74
  gags, 52, 137–138
  as goal of camp, 7
  group games, 146–154
  Hackey Sack, 74–75
  kite, 73–74
  letters to camp, 44–45
  Mad-Libs, 75
  magic tricks, 60–61
  for overcoming homesickness,
    39–40, 115–116
  packing games and activities, 39–40,
    59–62, 73–75
  paper and pencil games, 131–134
  puzzle books, 61, 74
  scary stories, 154–157
  skits, 157
  songs, 76–92
  sports equipment, 75
  tent-time activities, 119–127,
    136–137
  travel entertainment, 97–100
  travel games, 62
  water balloons, 75
Funny Feet, 124–125

G

Gags
  Chameleon Clothes, 138
  Freckle Face, 137
  hiding candy in tent, 52
  It's Contagious!, 138
  writing about, 188
Games. *See* Fun and games

Getting to and from camp. *See* Travel
Goals
   of camp, 7–8
   setting yours, 117–118
Golf
   Frisbee, 74
   nature, 150
"Gopher Guts" song, 83
Grass blade instrument, 163
Group games, 146–154
   Bug Hunt, 151
   Bug Race, 150–151
   Flashlight Tag, 147
   Franken-plant, 152–153
   Hike Hunt, 148
   Hunter!, 153
   Litter Hunt, 153
   Nature Golf, 150
   Quicksand!, 147
   Sock Scramble, 151
   Story Sounds, 154
   Touch and Tell, 152
   Tummy Ache, 147
   Winker, 149
Guilt about sending child to camp, 41

H

Hackey Sack, 74–75
Hair bands, 57
Hair dryer, 56
Hand Reading, 121–122
Hangman's Fortune, 132
Health forms, 54
Heat exhaustion, 195
Hidden Words game, 99
Hike Hunt game, 148
Hiking tips
   rules of the trail, 172
   what to take, 170–171
   what to watch for, 172–173
   what to watch out for, 173–174
   what to wear, 171
Hobbies, 61
"Hole in the Bottom of the Sea" song,
   84–85
Homesickness, 36–53. *See also* Separa-
   tion from home and family
   activities for overcoming, 39–40,
      114–118

boredom as cause of, 59, 114
   coping at camp, 39–41
   on first day at camp, 109
   as normal, 36–37, 110
   overcoming by making new friends,
      111–114
   perspective and, 118
   preparing your child for separation,
      37–39
   severe, signs of, 42–43
   talking about, 39, 109–110
   what not to do, 41–42
Hot Chocolate to Go, 70–71
Hot dog octopus, 142
Hunter! game, 153

I

Images of Nature activity, 162
Improvising
   pillow, 58
   tips for, 68
Independence, readiness for camp and,
   4–5
Insect bites, 199
Insect Study Kit, 104
Insurance forms, 54
It's Contagious! gag, 138

J

Jacks, 136
Jokes. *See also* Gags
   books of, 60
   for making friends, 112–113
   writing about, 188
Journal, 189–193
   "Best Friends" page, 192
   cutest boy/girl at camp in, 192
   daily entries, 189–190
   mementos in, 193
   names and addresses in, 191–192
   packing, 40–41, 61, 62
   remembering overlooked things,
      190–191
   special events in, 190
   things I love/dislike about camp in,
      192
   unforgettable moments in,
      190
   writing during quiet time, 116

K

Kamp Kabobs, 144
Keepsakes, 193
Kids-only versus family camps, 9–10
Kite, 73–74
"Kookaburra" song, 85–86
"Kumbaya" song, 86

L

"Lady with the Alligator Purse" song, 87
Laundry bag, 53
Laundry pen, marking everything with, 52
Laundry products, 53
Learning, as goal of camp, 7–8, 29–30
Leaves, pressed, 159
Length of camp session, 10
Letters to camp
  care packages, 40
  fun letters, 44–45
  mailing early, 44
  silly, 46
  smoothing the transition by, 43–44
  special surprises in, 45
Letters to home, 181–188
  address book for, 46
  fun abbreviations, 185–186
  funny signatures, 186
  others to write, 183
  overcoming homesickness through, 117
  to parents, 181–182
  prompts for, 47, 182–183
  special stationery for, 183–185, 186
  things to write about, 187–188
  "to be continued" letters, 186
Literary License game, 99
Litter Hunt game, 153
Loners, befriending, 113–114
Lovey, 63

M

Mad-Libs, 75
Magazines
  finding camps through, 22
  packing, 63
  Ranger Rick Magazine, 104

Magic tricks
  card tricks, 130–131
  Mind Reading, 122–123
  packing, 60–61
Mail. See Letters to camp; Letters to home
Map It! game, 99–100
Marbles, 136
Markers. See Pens and markers
Marking items with child's name, 52
Maturity, readiness for camp and, 4
Measles gag, 138
Mementos, 193
Messages, welcome back, 102
Mind Reading, 122–123
Mixed-Up Eights, 129
Money
  sending with child, 55
  stashing, 67–68
Morning Trail Mix, 71
Motion sickness, 94
Mystery Masterpiece activity, 166
"Mystery of the Missing Body Parts," 155–157

N

Nail Salon, 125
Names
  Camp Characters, 126–127
  funny signatures for letters, 186
  in journal, 191
  marking everything with, 52
  nicknames, 115
  travel safety and, 95
Nature Collections, 178–179
Nature crafts, 158–164. See also Arts and crafts
Nature Golf, 150
Nature images, 162
Nature Scavenger Hunt, 176
Necklace
  edible, 145
  flower, 161
Newspapers, finding camps through, 22
Nicknames, 115
Night Hike, 175–176
Nutty Fruity Balls, 71

O

Obeying the rules, 199–200
"On Top of Spaghetti" song, 88
Orange Muffins, 141

P

Packing
    activities for alone time, 39–40, 60
    address book, 46
    books, 64–67
    boredom busters, 39–40, 59–62,
        73–75
    child's involvement in, 49
    comforting favorites, 40, 63
    extras to include, 54–58
    first aid supplies, 53–54, 152
    forgotten items, 63–64
    games, 39–40, 59–62, 73–75
    hiding notes in suitcase, 45
    for hiking, 170–171
    improvising, 68
    items not to pack, 59
    journal, 40–41, 61, 62
    keeping things safe and dry, 69, 193
    marking all items, 52
    necessary items, 50–54
    personalizing the child's space, 67
    stashing valuables, 67–68
    stuff to keep handy, 69
    surprises, 62–63, 165
    treats and snacks, 69–73
    working together on, 33
Palm reading, 121–122
Paper and pencil games, 131–134
    Blind Dots and Boxes, 132–133
    Four-Letter Words, 133–134
    Hangman's Fortune, 132
    Triple Tic-Tac-Toe, 131
Paperwork, packing, 54
Party, welcome home surprise, 102
Peanut Butter Balls, 71
Pens and markers
    for Belly Button Art, 123
    for Body Tattoos, 124
    for Chin Chum, 126
    for Mystery Masterpiece, 166
    packing, 57

for Stone People, 168
    for Wacky Awards, 168–169
Personalized Plates game, 100
Personalizing the child's space, 67
Philosophy
    of the camp, 6
    of the camp director, 26
Phone calls
    arranging, 40
    during travel, 94, 95, 96
Physical skills learned at camp, 30
Pick a Card, Any Card trick, 130–131
Pillow
    improvising, 58
    packing, 50
Pillowcase
    decorating and signing, 100
    extra, 56
    improvising with, 68
    packing, 53
Pinecone Critters, 180
Pinecone Picture Holder, 162
Poison plants, 173, 196–197
Popcorn Trail Mix, 72
Potpourri, 163–164
Practice camping, 38
Pranks. See Gags
Preparing for camp, 28–47. See also
        Choosing a camp
    benefits of camp, 34–35
    campfire songs to learn, 76–92
    "Camp Video Night," 35
    checking out the camp, 32
    countdown calendar, 37
    experiences offered by camp, 29–31
    homesickness, 36–53
    packing, 33
    separation, preparing your child for,
        37–39
    sharing feelings, 33
    social skills needed, 5
    talking about camp, 33
    talking to the director, 32
    working together, 31–35
Pressed Flowers and Leaves, 159
Prompts
    for journal, 191–192
    for letters, 47, 182–183

Pros-and-cons list, 11–12
Puzzle books, 61, 74

Q

Questions
  for camp director, 26
  for making friends, 113
Quicksand! game, 147

R

Rainbow Row game, 100
Ranger Rick Magazine, 104
Rattlesnakes, 197–198
Readiness for camp
  determining, 4–5
  ideal age, 3
Recipes, 70–73, 139–145
  Apple Scramble, 141
  Baked Eggs, 144
  Banana Boats, 140
  Banana Chips, 70
  Bugs on a Log, 143
  Burrito Brunch, 143
  Crunchy Trail Mix, 71
  Edible Necklace, 145
  Eight-Legged Octopus, 142
  Fruit Leather, 70
  Hot Chocolate to Go, 70–71
  Kamp Kabobs, 144
  Morning Trail Mix, 71
  Nutty Fruity Balls, 71
  Orange Muffins, 141
  Peanut Butter Balls, 71
  Popcorn Trail Mix, 72
  S'Mores, 139–140
  Tiger Teeth, 145
  Tropical Trail Mix, 72
  UFO (unidentified frying object),
    143–144
  Walking Salad, 142
Re-creating camp at home, 103
Recreation centers, finding camps
    through, 21
Redecorating your child's room, 102
Red Riding Hood, 157
Registering for camp, 27
Resident camps versus day camps, 9
Rock City activity, 179
Role playing, as camp preparation, 38

Rules
  obeying, 199–200
  of the trail, 172

S

Safety issues
  animal bites, 199
  broken bones and sprains, 196
  camp as learning environment, 30
  choosing a camp, 25–26
  heat exhaustion, 195
  insect and bee stings, 199
  poisonous plants, 196–197
  reporting problems, 200
  scrapes and cuts, 195–196
  shock, 196
  snake bite, 187–188
  spider bites, 198–199
  sunstroke, 195
  ticks, 198
  for travel, 94–96
Scary stories, 154–157
Scavenger hunt, nature, 176
School, finding camps through, 22
Scrapbook, 61, 62, 116
Scrapes and cuts, 195–196
Scrunchies, packing, 57
Séance, 134
Security blanket, 40, 63
See-a-Sign game, 100
Self-sufficiency, readiness for camp
    and, 4–5
Separation from home and family. See
    also Homesickness
  benefits of camp experience,
    34–35
  confidence learned through, 31
  homesickness, 36–53
  as personal growth experience, 30
  preparing your child for, 37–39
  surviving, as goal of camp, 8
  worries about, 29, 33
Shadow Shapes, 135
Shock, 196
Shoes
  keeping burrs and stickers off,
    178
  for showers, 58
Shooting Star, 135

Shower shoes, 58
Shyness
    befriending loners, 113–114
    readiness for camp and, 5
Skits, 157
S'Mores, 139–140, 141
Snacks. *See* Food; Recipes
Snake bite, 187–188
Soap Carving, 167–168
Soap on a rope, packing, 56
Social skills
    learned at camp, 29–30
    readiness for camp and, 5
Socks, Funny Feet using, 124–125
Sock Scramble game, 151
Songs, 76–92
    "Annoying Song," 76
    "Ants Go Marching," 76–78
    "Baby Bumble Bee," 79
    "Backwards Song," 79
    "Be Kind to Your Fine-Feathered
        Friends," 80
    "Bingo!," 80
    "Boa Constrictor," 81
    "Cabin in the Woods," 81
    "Do Your Ears Hang Low?," 81–82
    "Found a Peanut," 82–83
    "Gopher Guts," 83
    "Hole in the Bottom of the Sea,"
        84–85
    "Kookaburra," 85–86
    "Kumbaya," 86
    "Lady with the Alligator Purse,"
        87
    "On Top of Spaghetti," 88
    "There's a Hole in My Bucket,"
        88–90
    "This Old Man," 90–91
    "Worms," 92
    "Worms Crawl In," 92
Spider bites, 198–199
Sports equipment, 75
Sprains, 196
Spray bottle with fan, 55
Star Search activity, 178
Stashing money and valuables, 67–68
Stationery for letters, 183–185, 186
Stings from insects and bees, 199
Stone People activity, 168

Stories
    camp-themed books, 64–67
    scary, 154–157
    telling using sounds, 154
Story Sounds game, 154
Structured versus flexible programs, 9
Sunstroke, 195
Surprise party (welcome home), 102

T
Talking
    about camp, 33
    about homesickness, 39, 109–110
    arranging phone calls, 40
    to camp director, 26, 32, 42
    Code One game, 136–137
    making new friends, 111–114
    promoting the camp too much, 41
    reporting problems, 200
Tank tops, 58
Tarantula, 199
Tattoos, temporary, 124
Teddy bear, 63
Tent fun, 119–138
    activities, 119–127
    card games, 127–129
    card tricks, 130–131
    flashlight fun, 134–135
    gags, 137–138
    games to play with tent mates,
        136–137
    paper and pencil games, 131–134
Tent-time activities, 119–127
    Belly Button Art, 123
    Body Tattoos, 124
    Camp Characters, 126–127
    Chin Chum, 126
    Fortune Telling, 120–121
    Funny Feet, 124–125
    Hand Reading, 121–122
    Mind Reading, 122–123
    Nail Salon, 125
    other games, 136–137
That's Your Card trick, 130
"There's a Hole in My Bucket" song,
    88–90
"This Old Man" song, 90–91
Ticks, 198
Tic-Tac-Toe, triple, 131

Tiger Teeth, 145
Time and timing. *See also* First day at camp
  countdown calendar, 37
  first day at camp, 109–118
  ideal age for camp, 3
  readiness for camp, 4–5
  registering for camp, 27
"To be continued" letters, 186
Toiletries, 51
Toiletry bag, 51
Touch and Tell game, 152
Towels, 50–51
Tracking the Trail activity, 174–175
Trail activities, 170–180
  Birdseed Pinecone Feeders, 177–178
  Blazing a Trail, 180
  Blind Walk, 176
  Dinosaur Bones, 177
  Follow the Floater, 179
  Follow the Map, 175
  hiking tips, 170–174
  Nature Collections, 178–179
  Nature Scavenger Hunt, 176
  Night Hike, 175–176
  Pinecone Critters, 180
  Rock City, 179
  Star Search, 178
  Tracking the Trail, 174–175
Trail mix
  crunchy, 71
  morning, 71
  packing, 63
  popcorn, 72
  tropical, 72
Travel
  air travel tips, 96
  bus travel tips, 95–96
  car travel tips, 95
  entertainment on the way, 97–100
  motion sickness, 94
  safety issues, 94–96
  welcoming your child home, 101–103

Travel entertainment, 97–100
  Alphabet Adventure, 97
  Animal Hunt, 98
  Backseat Bingo, 98
  Counting Cars, 98
  Fifty States, 98–99
  Hidden Words, 99
  Literary License, 99
  Map It!, 99–100
  Personalized Plates, 100
  Rainbow Row, 100
  See-a-Sign, 100
Treats. *See* Food; Recipes
Triple Tic-Tac-Toe, 131
Tropical Trail Mix, 72
Truth or Dare cards, 122
T-shirts, oversized, 57
Tummy Ache game, 147
Twig Creatures activity, 159

U

UFO (unidentified frying object), 143–144
Universities, finding camps through, 22

V

Valuables, stashing, 67–68
Videos, 35
Visiting the camp, 39

W

Wacky Awards, 168–169
Wacky War, 127–128
Walking Salad, 142
War card game, wacky, 127–128
Water balloons, 75
Water moccasins, 197–198
Web sites
  camp fairs information, 22
  for specific camps, 18–21
Welcoming your child home, 101–103
Wildlife Booklet, 104
Winker game, 149
"Worms Crawl In" song, 92
"Worms" song, 92